The Dev Lead Trenches

by Chris Tankersley

The Dev Lead Trenches

Contents Copyright ©2017–2018 Chris Tankersley—All Rights Reserved

Book and cover layout, design and text Copyright ©2020 musketeers.me, LLC. and its predecessors—All Rights Reserved. Print and Digital copies available from <https://www.phparch.com/books/>.

php[architect] edition published: February 2020

Print ISBN:	978-1-940111-71-1
PDF ISBN:	978-1-940111-72-8
ePub ISBN:	978-1-940111-73-5
Mobi ISBN	978-1-940111-74-2

Produced & Printed in the United States

No part of this book may be reproduced, stored in a public retrieval system, or publicly transmitted in any form or by means without the prior written permission of the publisher, except in the case of brief quotations embedded in critical reviews or articles.

Disclaimer

Although every effort has been made in the preparation of this book to ensure the accuracy of the information contained therein, this book is provided "as-is" and the publisher, the author(s), their distributors and retailers, as well as all affiliated, related or subsidiary parties take no responsibility for any inaccuracy and any and all damages caused, either directly or indirectly, by the use of such information. We have endeavored to properly provide trademark information on all companies and products mentioned in the book by the appropriate use of capitals. However, we cannot guarantee the accuracy of such information.

musketeers.me, the musketeers.me logo, php[architect], the php[architect] logo are trademarks or registered trademarks of musketeers.me, LLC, its assigns, partners, predecessors and successors.

All other trademarks are the property of the respective owners.

Written by
Chris Tankersley

Managing Editor
Oscar Merida

Editor
Kara Ferguson

Published by
musketeers.me, LLC.
4627 University Dr
Fairfax, VA 22030 USA

240-348-5PHP (240-348-5747)
<info@phparch.com>
<www.phparch.com>

Table of Contents

1. So Now You're a Team Lead — 1
    The Accidental Team Lead — 2
    Let's Be on a Team — 4

2. Dealing With People — 5
    Learn to Talk To People — 5
    Be Firm and Confident — 6
    Think Win-Win, Not Win-Lose — 7
    The Dark Side — 8
    Communication Is Key — 9

3. What Not To Do — 11
    Spending Too Much Time Coding — 11
    Letting the Team Self Govern — 12
    Making All the Decisions — 13
    Analysis Paralysis — 14
    Letting Pride and Ego Get in the Way — 15

TABLE OF CONTENTS

4. Project Management Toolbox — 17
- Old School Pen and Paper — 18
- Communication — 18
- Calendars — 19
- Tracking Projects — 20
- Staying Organized Is Not Hard — 21

5. Simple Project Management — 23
- Methodologies — 23
- Some Design Up Front — 25
- Scheduling — 26
- Stick It on a Board — 27
- The Retrospective and Restart the Cycle — 29
- Simple Project Management for an Easier Workday — 29

6. How Long Will It Take? — 31
- Divide and Conquer — 32
- Lies…I Mean Numbers — 33
- Your Estimates Are Wrong — 34
- Estimates Are Not Deadlines — 35
- Estimates Are Important — 35

7. Issue Workflows for Teams — 37
- Create an Issue — 38
- Triage — 40
- Sprint Planning — 41
- Working an Issue — 41
- Reviewing the PR — 44
- Completing the Merge — 44

8. From Issues to Code   45

    Origin, Upstream, and Forks   45
    From a Good Base   46
    Branching Out   47
    Working on Branches   48
    The Pull Request   49
    Merging and Deleting   49
    Releasing   50
    An Enjoyable Workflow   50

9. Reviewing Code   51

    Code Review Tools   52
    Code Review in Practice   55
    Now Start Reviewing Code   56

10. Finding Someone New   57

    Describing the Job   57
    Building a Network   59
    Going Through Resumes   60
    The First Interview   61
    The Second Interview   61
    The Offer   62
    Onboarding   63

TABLE OF CONTENTS

11. Coming Aboard! — 65
Be Organized — 66
The Hardware and Software — 66
Assign a Buddy — 67
Getting Going — 68
Code Reviews — 69
Better Productivity Through Better Onboarding — 69

12. Measuring Success — 71
Useless Metrics — 71
SMART — 72
OKRs — 73
360-Degree Peer Reviews — 74
Discovering and Dealing With Poor Performance — 74
What Works Best — 76

13. The Code Monkey — 77
The Argument — 77
Dealing with Problems is Key — 79
The Middle of the Road — 80
Communication Helps — 81

14. The Talk — 83
Before The Talk — 84
Having The Talk — 85
Following Through — 86
It Sucks — 87

15. Burning Out — 89
- Detecting Burnout — 90
- Avoiding Burnout — 90
- Burnout Versus Depression — 93
- Getting Better — 93

16. It's Toxic — 95
- Poor Work-Life Balance — 96
- Toxic Management — 97
- Stifling Creativity — 98
- Going Green — 98

17. Ongoing Education — 101
- Getting a Budget — 102
- Conferences — 103
- Online Training — 104
- Dead Trees… I mean Books — 105
- Encouragement — 106

18. Creating a Culture — 107
- What Culture Is Not — 108
- Keys to a Real Company Culture — 109
- Go Forth and Run Your Team — 111

Index — 113

Editor's Note

This book collects almost two-years worth of writings based on Chris Tankersley's experience leading development teams. He first wrote these in his column, also named "The Dev Lead Trenches," for php[architect] magazine. Chris' approach to managing a group of programmers comes from the experiences only another programmer can appreciate. His advice is grounded in an authentic concern for bringing the best out people without treating them as interchangeable cogs. He recognizes the value of well-defined, shared workflows without advocating blind adherence to bureaucratic processes. Whether you're a seasoned lead developer or have just been "promoted" to the role, this collection can help you nurture an expert programming team within your organization.

This book re-organizes his essays thematically, instead of including them in chronological publication order.

- Chapters 1–3 touch upon what the Development Lead role should entail, how to interact with others, and also defines what you should not do.
- Chapters 4–9 look at aspects of managing what your team is tasked with, from project management advice to a workflow for turning feature or bug tickets into deployable code.
- Chapters 10–14 deal with the personnel aspects of finding new hires, assessing individuals, and handling poor performance.
- Chapter 15–18 tackle topics related to your team, or company, culture with advice on what contributes to a positive one and the things to avoid to prevent burnout and toxicity in your workplace.

If you're a newly minted lead, start with chapter one to get your bearings. Otherwise, each chapter can stand alone if you have a specific need for help or insight.

While I've revised the copy from past articles, I did not change the essence of any section. I primarily updated the language to flow as part of a book, replacing mentions of previous articles with links to chapters within this book.

Chapter 1

So Now You're a Team Lead

I never planned on being a team lead.

I'll take that back. If anyone assumes, in their career, they will never lead a team of anything, then they are not really in a career. They are just in a job. Which is fine; you be you.

I never planned on being a team lead when it happened. Way back in 2008 was the first time I was in charge of something, and that something was the web infrastructure and software for an insurance company. I doubt I was an outstanding team lead, though realistically I was just the most senior developer. I began the job as the guy working on the website, but I had a knack for networking as well. After a few years, our applications had grown in complexity and number, and I needed a coworker.

We hired someone who was just getting into programming, and PHP was a relatively new language for him. I was doing more and more architecture work, but I was still in charge of the main web applications and hardware. So I took him under my wing and did my best to show him what I thought were good practices. I wanted to do for him what I had not had done for me. I had gone to school and learned from some excellent teachers but never had someone show me the ropes on a job.

Looking back now, I realize I was mentoring him. Much of it was because I am a very lazy man, so the more I taught him, the fewer questions I had to answer and the more work he could do on his own. I did honestly want him to succeed, though, because I was overworked and was moving into more of an architectural role. I wanted to leave my code in good hands.

I pushed him to not always automatically agree with me and to go to conferences. I learned how to deal with the politics of the office so we could get suitable hardware. I wanted him to experiment, to learn, and to fail on his own. I don't ever remember him failing but stumbling in a good way. The kind where, when you stand back up, you learned why you stumbled, and not because I was yelling at him for screwing up.

Fast forward to my current job. I was specifically hired to run our web UI team, and part of that is leading an honest-to-goodness team. At this point, I have led a few teams, but my current team is the size I enjoy. We have someone working on the JavaScript frontend, another working on the actual design and layout, myself, and a new hire.

Our new hire is a good friend of mine. I've known her for a few years, and she's far from a junior dev. One day she messaged me that she was having some problems with a pull request. Something was just not working right when she was pushing code up. I will admit we have kind of a janky workflow at the moment, but looking in GitHub, she had somehow duplicated all of the commits in master and pushed it up to the central repository. Pull requests that were waiting now looked all sorts of funky.

I logged in, pulled down another copy of the master from our other coworker, and did a force push back up. All fixed. She and I then set to work figuring out what happened.

I wasn't mad. Thankfully, the distributed nature of Git makes it incredibly easy to have multiple backups of repositories sitting around, so I was never in a state of panic. People joke all the time about deleting a production database and the fallout, but this did not even come close. I *have* deleted production databases before—during the workday. S**t hits the fan *really* quick. We took it in stride, and we figured out what happened.

The Accidental Team Lead

At some point in your programming career, you will become a team lead, either formally or informally. Your title might be *Lead Developer*, *Dev Lead*, *Programming Manager*, or even *Programmer*. If you find yourself suddenly charged with making decisions for a group of people, congratulations! You are now a Team Lead.

I want to do for you what I did for the first coworker I led all those years ago. No one taught me how to be a team lead, just like no one taught me how to program in PHP. As with any job, there will be differences between what each team lead does, but I feel all team leads have a core set of responsibilities they will need to do. Most of them will have nothing at all to do with programming and everything to do with people. I am still learning myself, and I stumble every so often. As long as you are willing to learn and learn from your mistakes, you will be a great team lead.

Throughout the subsequent articles in this column, I will touch on the following ideas and more. Since this is my first time writing about being a team lead, and hopefully, you, as a reader, want to learn right away, here are a few of the things you need to consider as a team lead.

Communication Is Key

I am a remote developer, so this hits a few deep points with me, but as a team lead you need to make sure communication is open between you and the people you work with. You will be the one in charge of making sure deadlines are understood both between the team and upper management. You will be the one that needs to know when problems arise. You need to know when your team is blocked and needs something.

Don't be the kind of lead that only talks to the team at meetings. A good lead will be right there with the rest of the team, talking to them on a daily basis. Daily standup meetings are helpful, but you want to be available and listen when there are problems or there are needs. Make sure your team has the tools to communicate. Have e-mail, chat, and verbal conversations when appropriate.

Many programmers are introverts and find it hard to talk to groups of people. One-on-one communication may be more comfortable. As a team lead you will need to overcome that in whatever way works for you. You need to listen. Make sure your team knows they can talk to you—and even question you.

Communication goes both ways. You need to work with your team to translate management's needs and wishes to the team. Effective written and verbal communication is critical.

Above all, be respectful in your communication. We are all adults and deserve to be treated as such, even if the other person is wrong.

Help The Team Grow

It will be your job as a team lead to make sure your team is growing. Well-oiled development teams are the ones with the ability to use whatever best practices are in the marketplace at the time. Your team will be stronger knowing they can grow in their skills and not stagnate. Experimentation is vital, even if you do not dedicate specific time to research and development.

You need to help the team grow. Work with upper management to make sure a training budget is available. Find a way to send team members to conferences, either as attendees or speakers depending on experience. There are plenty of regional conferences around the US, and Europe has a handful of excellent conferences to attend.

Encourage reading and watching videos on new topics. Sign up for services like Laracasts or whatever would be equivalent for your programming stack. Find new tools, and let your team find new tools that make their jobs easier and more productive. Allow the team to find what works for them.

While you don't have to accept every single idea under the sun, at least let the team try new things, and have chances to learn new things.

Shield the Team

You will be the first line of defense from management. That sounds harsh, but the reality is that even the best managers are still managers.

1. So Now You're a Team Lead

I work with a great team and have a fantastic manager, but there are times when feature requests and bugs make it onto our issue board which, well, shouldn't be there. In meetings, you are a representative of your team and will be the one dealing with requests.

Learning to work with management and keep them at arm's length from the rest of the team is a good thing. You are a liaison, but also a filter. You get to deal with management, schedules, and budgets, so other people on the team do not have to. Part of your job is now to keep your team focused and productive. I sit through an entire Monday's worth of meetings, which I would not wish on anyone else on my team.

If features are not going to be met by the deadline, you are the one informing the other teams and management. You might be on the team, but as its lead, you are the voice of the team.

Stand Up for the Team

As a liaison between upper management and the team, it is also your responsibility to stand up for your team. If deadlines are not reasonable, learning to push back is a must. Put on your project management hat and work with management and teams to find solutions, but always keep in mind your team is made up of people who assume you are working with, and for, them.

You are the one that will need to make requests for hardware, for conferences, and for better deadlines. Make sure praise is not kept inside the team but shared upward.

A good team lead will work to remove roadblocks for the team whenever possible. It might be hard, and you will not always win, but you must try.

Let's Be on a Team

I want to help you grow as a team lead, whether you took a job as a team lead want to do better, or were like me and all of a sudden in charge of other people. Ultimately, it is not as scary as one might think, but being a team lead may mean getting outside of your comfort zone.

As these columns continue, I will expand upon the few ideas I mentioned before and more. I want to share my stories with you as an actual team lead on various teams so you can learn from my mistakes. I want to give you the tools to effectively manage your team and to help your team members grow.

As a sneak peek for the next chapter, consider this—don't tell your coworker a monkey could do a better job than them.

Chapter 2

Dealing With People

A large part of being a team lead is communication, and being the first line of communication for your team to outside parties. These parties could be internal, like a C-level executive, or a representative for a larger team in which your team is but a section of. The parties can also be external to the company such as vendors, clients, or service providers. You will more than likely have to deal with a combination of these groups, as most of them vie for your team's time and resources.

Your team will also have their wants and needs. This can be software and tools to do their job, hardware, time off, requests for deadline extensions, and a whole host of other things. You'll need to relay these to outside parties. Remember, you are the buffer.

Oh, and you have to keep everyone happy.

Learn to Talk To People

Step one in getting what you want is learning to talk to people. Even then, it's learning to talk and engage with others. You have to be a people person, and not just so the engineers don't have to deal with people, which means actually talking to people and listening.

2. Dealing With People

I wish I had a specific book or technique that works wonders, but I don't. All I have is my personal experience.

The first thing I did was to be sociable with people in my department —even the Code Monkey. Well, as much as I could anyway. I learned the kinds of things they liked to do on the weekends. I tried to find common ground. One coworker of mine was really into weight lifting, something I have no interest in. I listened to him explain his workout regime and the things he was doing. While it did not become a passion of mine, I still listened. Engaging this way made it easier to talk about something I enjoyed, and I tried to relate it to things I knew.

One of my bosses was into older cars, which is something I was, and am, very into. Talking with my boss became much more comfortable when I could break the ice before launching into something work-related. It set both of us at ease and somewhat put us on the same ground.

After that, I did the same thing to people outside of our office. While waiting for files to download, I would look around for something to ask. One of the easiest ways to start a conversation is just to ask questions. This technique is a great way to initiate small talk without feeling like you need to do the bulk of the talking. I would look for pictures of kids or family, sports teams, books on their desk, something to trigger a conversation. Some people did not want to talk, but at least I tried.

As part of this, you need to also listen to their responses. If you are just making small talk to fill a void, they will notice. Engage in conversation and converse.

It sucked. It still does, to this day. I hate talking to people some days, but learning to talk to people is the best thing I've ever learned to do.

Be Firm and Confident

When it comes to communication, confidence is vital. If you are shaky in your convictions or position, the other person will pick up on it. If you are trying to push back on a deadline, be firm and clear in your reasoning.

One of the first things I learned when getting into network security was social engineering. Social engineering boils down to the idea that if you are confident, people will believe you. Consider the classic hacker scenario where someone shows up wearing a jumpsuit with a clipboard and asks for access to a network closet to do maintenance. There is an excellent chance that if you are acting confident about the situation and what you are doing, someone will let you in. I know it works because I once had a phone technician all of a sudden in a server room that no one told IT about.

Now, the phone tech was not lying about why he was there, and I am not advocating you do that. What I am advocating is that you need to be sure of what you want. If you sound confident, people will take you more seriously.

Never be afraid to push back and say, "No." I am amazed by how many people will never say "no" to someone else, especially if that person is above them in the hierarchy. You do not have to belligerent, but you can be firm.

Let's take the deadline example. If your deadline is to finish the project in two weeks, but you have four weeks of work, you either need to push back the deadline or drop work. Having a death march is a last resort, and honestly, something I never put on the table.

Talk with your team and decide on the best course of action. Remember, you and your team were hired to not only do the work but also be responsible enough to do your job correctly, which includes coming up with contingency plans.

So, your team decides they need to push back to the schedule because the remaining work is too important. You need the extra time to release a complete application.

When you go to the person in charge of moving the deadline, be firm in your position. Explain why you need to push the deadline back. If you trust your team, then you have made a good decision, and you should be confident in it.

If your boss or whomever the stakeholder is, pushes back, stay firm. Say "no" and give reasons for why you are pushing back. Be stubborn in the outcome you want, but you do not have to be stubborn in your attitude. There will be back and forth, and there are only three outcomes—you get what you want, you don't, or you compromise. Honestly, sometimes that third option is the best.

Think Win-Win, Not Win-Lose

Remember, nothing about negotiating or dealing with people needs to be a win-lose situation. Breaking free of zero-sum thinking, or the general idea of "your gain is my loss," is an incredibly tall but necessary hurdle you must overcome. Learn to compromise, and you will find that more often than not, you still get something close to what you want.

Start by trying to understand why someone does not agree with you. In the case of pushing back the deadline, there may be a very valid reason for postponing the deadline. After you have given your position on why the deadline *must* be pushed back, listen to the other side on why it *cannot* be pushed back. I mean actively listen, and consider those wants.

The other party is not necessarily trying to undermine you or your position. Sometimes your needs just do not align with the other party's needs. When that happens, you need to find common ground.

Get into the other person's shoes. Maybe there is a client deadline that cannot be pushed back, like a full-page ad in a major newspaper. Your position to move the deadline is now up against a hard deadline. You will need to give a little. What you give up is part of the negotiation, but realizing it is not a tit-for-tat situation helps both sides.

Maybe some features that you think are important can be slipped. Perhaps a short-term solution can be put in place while finishing the final application behind the scenes. Talk and work with the other party. You both have the best interests of the project in mind. Remember, you and your team are here to solve business problems, just like everyone else.

2. Dealing With People

There is no hard or fast rule for compromising and negotiating. The main things I suggest is having empathy for the other party and removing the need to "win" an argument. Sometimes a compromise is all that is needed.

The Dark Side

There is one area of communication and wrangling many people do not ever want to talk about, let alone deal with. That is the dreaded topic of "office politics." Just the term sounds back-stabby, and for many employees, they look at office politics as a real-life Game of Thrones, which is not a healthy approach for anyone trying to work together. In a way it is, but you can deal with office politics without all the bloodbath—although more dragons in the workplace would be kind of neat.

The notion, by itself, is not a bad thing. Office politics is simply a broad term for understanding and using the organization structure, personal influences, and assets that are available to a person. You *could* go down the path of office gossip and turning departments against each other, but you don't *have* to. I don't recommend it anyway. I will give you a good example.

The Server Purchase

At a previous job, none of the departments officially had a budget. Everyone was told if you needed something, you just had to ask for it. The idea was that it was up to the department head to be the gatekeeper and make sure money was not misspent. On paper, it sounds like a good idea, but at the end of the year, departments spending too much money without justification were obviously told to spend less the next year.

Knowing this, and knowing that ultimately hardware purchases would come down to how much it would cost, I drew up a prospectus for a new Storage Area Network (SAN). We had invested heavily in virtualization, but each set of virtual machines ran on individual computers. Without a backend storage solution, any virtual machine on that host was completely down until we built a new host. That could mean a few hours to a few days. A SAN would allow us to do hot-swapping of virtual machines between hosts.

It would be costly. A full SAN would have run roughly $20,000 between hardware and our regular service contracts. That is a lot of money. I did two things—one was to scale back. I did not have to buy the SAN full of drives, so I knocked the order down to something sensible—five 500GB drives to run in a RAID'd LUN. That brought the cost down quite a bit. Step one of office politics was understanding that "no budget" did not mean we could spend endlessly.

Step two of office politics was knowing my audience. I not only had to be mindful of my spending, but I had to make this sound like a good deal, both now and in the long run. I did this by comparing the amount of storage we had in machines we usually purchased, which were 2U servers, and that we could buy less onboard storage for each device. 1U servers could be even cheaper than 2Us! I would save us hundreds of dollars on each server we purchased!

Why didn't I just explain the technical reasons I listed above as to why we needed the SAN? I did, but I also knew I had to sweeten the deal. If I could show we could save money in the long run, the purchase had a better chance of getting approved. We could legitimately buy less onboard storage, but I knew I had to hype those savings over the technical reasons.

Making Friends

You do not have to be best friends with everyone, but being on everyone's good side does not hurt. At any job, I make sure to talk to the other departments. I don't allow them to cut corners, but I do try not to ignore anyone. When I was working in a more help desk role early in my career, something as simple as making small talk helped get rid of the stigma that all IT people were unsociable gremlins in a dark office.

I tried and was nice to people. I listened. That grew relationships and trust. I stopped getting the run around when it came to diagnosing problems as other people realized I was just there to help, not judge. Did I think some of the things were completely stupid? I sure did. I just did not let it get in the way of having a good working relationship with coworkers and people in other departments.

When I advanced in my career, being kind to people and helping make sure their needs were met was not a sinister goal; it was one of mutual understanding. If we all worked together, everything goes much more smoothly. Being friendly, but understanding the other person's viewpoint and motivation goes a long way.

Communication Is Key

I harp on communication because it truly is at the heart of being a team lead. Dealing with people is one of the greatest skills anyone can learn. It is not just because you want to manipulate people, but it is about fostering trust and collaboration between people.

It is much easier in the short term to be an ass to people, but in the long run, you will have a bad time. Learn to talk to people, learn to listen to people, and learn to understand people—those are some of the hardest but most worthwhile things you will ever learn.

2. Dealing With People

Chapter 3

What Not To Do

We'll discuss all of the things you should be doing as a technical and developer lead. You should learn to work with the other departments and figureheads; you should be protecting your team, you should be improving working conditions both from a developer perspective and an environmental aspect. There are many things that you should be doing, and I hope my advice is helpful.

Let's talk about some of the things you should *not* be doing. These are some of the habits and problems I have observed as developers move into the more managerial role a lead developer is. These habits are not hard to break once you identify them, but the trick comes in being able to recognize them. I hope these are as helpful as the list of things you should be doing.

Spending Too Much Time Coding

Back in college, I had a choice between doing network engineering or computer programming. I decided to go into computer programming because I did not like all the physical work of lugging equipment around, running cable, or having to do inventory. I did plenty of the lugging and inventory in retail jobs, and while I can run cable, I prefer not to do it. I elected to get into a field where I can put on my headphones and work for hours at a time in my little world.

3. What Not To Do

This decision was reinforced when I took one of my first "corporate" jobs. I did double duty working on the networking team and working on our applications. I *hated* the networking aspect of it, but not because of the physical work; I found the networking part boring. Once you have set up a few networks, it becomes easy to identify the pitfalls to watch out for and the support structures you need in place. I had a reliable vendor to buy hardware from who did not give me guff. I had logging, metrics, and reports automatically emailed to me, and once a server was up, I rarely ever did more than necessary maintenance.

Coding is a much more enjoyable job for me. After programming for almost fourteen years, I still love the programming aspect of my work. Putting on the headphones and creating something from just words and frustration is one of the most rewarding things I still do.

Being a lead developer or a technical lead means you will be doing more manager and project management work. You no longer get to spend nearly all of your time coding. A strong technical lead has a healthy and sound development background, and they should know the ins-and-outs of development work. By becoming a lead developer, you are willing to use that experience and knowledge in areas outside of programming and development.

I estimate I spend only about fifty to sixty percent of my time doing real development work. If you were to look at my progress on a burn-down chart, I would have a low velocity. That is not because I am a slow developer; it is because I have to split my time between actual development and the other areas of my job. I am lucky it is not all meetings, but I do have to do code reviews, planning, working with other teams, and some general management stuff.

You will have to make sure not to bury yourself under issues or spend all your time developing. It is tempting to think you can get away with doing a bunch of development because you have a strong team, or you have streamlined processes to the point you have a bunch of extra time. There will always be something else you need to focus on because you do not want to fall into the next item.

Letting the Team Self Govern

I try to be a mostly hands-off lead. I know how annoying it is to have a manager continually bugging you about progress, sticking their head in at the most inopportune times while you are trying to work. Those TPS reports will get done on time, and it does not matter if I do them now or in an hour, Bob. Leave me alone.

My current team at work is pretty self-sufficient, which is something I love. I know I can give them issues to work on from the project board, and at the end of a sprint, we usually have things done. They can ask questions when needed, and they can find information on their own. I enjoy steering the ship and making sure we are on the correct course instead of having to constantly check up on them and make sure they are on task.

You have to watch out for getting into a groove where you assume a team will take care of itself. Your job as a lead developer is to help steer the ship, but part of that job is to make sure the ship runs as it should. You have to make sure the correct work is getting done, and getting done by the deadline. You do have the ability to push back on deadlines, but once you have agreed to one, you need to make sure it is followed. A ship is not going to magically work if the engine crew decides to stop working for the week and ignore problems.

I am a bit of a pessimist, but you cannot rely on everyone to fix their problems—some of them may be self-made, some of them may be your fault, and some of them might be due to external factors. You can help with the last two by making sure you are engaged with the team and actively trying to solve problems. Putting on your headphones and checking in with the team once a week is not going to work.

You do not have to be overbearing, but you do need to check up on people. If you can get away with it, check in via Slack or email. I never expect an immediate response through either, but the less intrusive you can be, the better. If they are not answering, then you may have to be a bit more direct, either going to their desk, phone call, or video chat. I always try to let people update me at their own pace, but if someone is consistently ignoring you, or it always takes multiple pokes, then there is a problem.

You may also be called upon to handle disputes. There are plenty of times I bemoan when people seem to find it hard to act like adults and deal with their problems, but at some point, you will need to step in and play mediator. If two teammates are disagreeing, you should be there to help diffuse the situation or be there to help sort out the problem. I am all for advocating saying, "try and sort it out yourself," as I do to my kids, but as the ship's captain, you need to be there to make final decisions.

Making All the Decisions

This habit is the opposite of letting the team self-govern. Part of being a lead developer is helping to come up with decisions, workflows, and implementations, but you do not want to be a tyrant in those decisions. When you work on a team, you need to work with the team when it comes to making decisions. You should not be hiring drones that do everything you say just because you say it.

Teams should include people from different backgrounds, experiences, and expertise. While you may have the final say on how something is built, do not fall into the trap of ignoring all of the knowledge the team has when it comes to making decisions. When someone comes to your team with a new feature, do not make a snap judgment. Get the team together and talk it over. Someone may come up with a better idea than what you have in your head or may bring up something you did not consider.

A good example of this is a project I am currently working on. We are developing a management tool to allow remotely configuring multiple machines from a single interface. This approach all works fine since we are API-first, but then my coworker realized our logging system would not show names properly when we are remotely managing. It would only show the name for the API key being used. We needed to come up with a better solution to properly log change management.

At a previous job, we had a new feature that broke our backups. This bug went unnoticed for about a month. It was due to one person deciding how something should work (not me, thankfully) without consulting with the rest of the team. There was no consideration for how the new feature would impact existing installs or existing features; a decision was made on the spot due to it coming from "higher up."

Unless you must make a decision immediately, take the time to talk with the team and listen to them. Your word may be final, but you can make sure that the option you choose comes from an informed decision.

Analysis Paralysis

Now that I touted taking the time to sit down and make a decision, I am going to caution against taking that to an extreme. An informed decision is a decision with some thought, information, and context behind it. However, there is such a thing as too much information. When you're confronted with an enormous amount of decisions or ideas, it can lead to a phenomenon known as "analysis paralysis." You become so overwhelmed with your options that you end up not acting.

A lead developer needs to make decisions. That is one of the core concepts of the job. A lead developer has a wealth of knowledge they can pull from to help make gut decisions, and those decisions should be tempered by information from your team. You need to make a decision, and you cannot be overwhelmed by the information at your disposal.

Suppose your team is tasked with implementing a new content management system for an internal tool. You could use WordPress, you could use Drupal, you could use PyroCMS, you could use SilverStripe, Grav, BigTree, concrete5, or one of the other tens of PHP-based systems available at the moment. They all have their advantage and disadvantages, and as the lead developer, you need to make a decision on which to use. There are so many out there that it can be tough to make a decision. And when it is tough to make a decision, you might not make one at all.

Trust your gut. Collect basic information and go from there. What is your team most familiar with? We recently decided to redo our blog and main website at work, and at first, we went with a static site solution. The blog was done in Sculpin because that was the quickest way to get it out the door, and because all of the authors using it were developers with a Git-based editing workflow. We set up an auto-deploy, and all the writers had to do was just push to master to update the site.

For the corporate website, we ended up with a Drupal website. The corporate site needed to be updated by non-developers (or at least ones that did not want to muck around with raw HTML 90 percent of the time). While there are a ton of content management solutions out there, our team was most familiar with Wordpress and Drupal. Drupal won out because down the line, some of the features we want would be easier to implement due to our familiarity with Drupal. Also, as a security company, the last thing we wanted was a compromised WordPress site—my boss's words, not mine.

For both sites, there were a good few weeks where no decision was made on which way to go. Finally, I made the decision, and we pulled it into our team to handle.

You also have to be careful not to waste time waiting for information. While this did not come up when redoing the websites, we receive feature requests from customers which create situations where we are constantly waiting for information. You cannot wait forever to make a decision, and you may have to decide without all of the data. It is your job to gather the knowledge to make decisions with what you have. Try and get as much information as possible in your timeframe, but you may have times where there isn't much info to work with.

Letting Pride and Ego Get in the Way

I am going to leave you with one final thing to watch out for. Being a lead developer means leaving your ego at the door. You may be in the position because you have the most experience or the best management skills, but that does not mean you are infallible. You will make mistakes. You will need to own up to those mistakes. You will make bad decisions. It is up to you to continue to keep the ship sailing toward the goals management puts forth. Work with your team, not against your team. Know when to ask for their help, and be available when they need yours.

I am never one for singling out an individual or throwing someone under the bus. Those are issues you can handle with your team without letting the wider world know---though, as I'll mention in other chapters, sometimes you will need to deal with issues, including <u>terminations</u>. Your team will hopefully function better knowing they will not be a direct target, and feel safer owning up to their own mistakes.

Chapter 4

Project Management Toolbox

Let's dive into some of the different tools I use on a day-to-day basis. Many of the tools are project management related, but some are just nice things to keep me organized overall.

Being organized is crucial as it is up to you, as the face of the team and the one working with outside groups, to keep track of what is going on. You will be responsible for communicating dates and information to your team and others, and to make sure everyone has the information they need.

One of the best ways to help avoid burnout and that "death march" feeling is to stay organized, and notice when something is not going as scheduled. If you're disorganized, you will have a hard time keeping things on track or may not realize when work starts to slip.

I primarily use Linux and Android, so most of the software is either web-based or open source. I will try to point out similar software on other platforms where I can, but many of the tools should run on just about anything.

Old School Pen and Paper

Much of my day-to-day planning is handled via pen and paper. This habit has more to do with the flexibility that a physical medium gives me over an electronic one, and you may be different. I have not yet found software that matches the speed and organization of a paper-based system.

Overall, I tend to use a bullet journaling[1] system. It is a light-weight tracking system that relies on daily and monthly lists of things to do. You mark items with specific icons, like a bullet to denote a task, a circle to indicate an event, and a dash to signify notes.

Each day you write down the things you do in a list and cross them off as you finish them. Things that do not get finished migrate to the next day. Things like notes eventually get lumped together in their lists, called collections.

It is a very quick and easy system to get started with, and all you need is a notebook and a pen.

There are a ton of different types of notebooks out there. My favorite is the Leuchtturm 1917 notebook[2], which is a notebook that comes in a few different sizes. I use the dotted A5 version, but it comes in a ruled and squared versions as well. I feel the dotted layout gives more flexibility when it comes to layouts.

When selecting a notebook, I highly recommend one that has nice, acid-free paper. Not only will the pages last longer if you ever have to go back and look something up, but they also tend to write better. Moleskine is another excellent brand of notebooks that come in a variety of sizes and layouts.

For actually writing, I use a Staedtler Triplus[3], a very fine-tipped felt pen. In the Leuchtturm, it is possible to see it through the page just a bit, but it does not bleed. It writes smoothly and consistently.

Whatever you end up using, I highly suggest looking into bullet journaling as a task-tracking system. Each morning I look at what remains from the previous day and move it forward. On Mondays, I also sync my calendar items, since Monday is generally my meeting and planning day. If you keep everything up-to-date, it does not take much time at all.

Communication

Communication with a team is vital. For better or for worse, the communication realm has boiled down to a few choice applications that work decently well for everyone.

For instant messaging, the reigning champion is Slack. Unless your company has a compelling reason to self-host chat, Slack, for better or for worse, is one of the better tools. Mattermost[4] has positioned itself as an open-source alternative, but they have multi-factor authentication gated behind their paid tier.

---

[1] bullet journaling: http://bulletjournal.com
[2] Leuchtturm 1917 notebook: https://amazon.com/dp/B002CVAU1Y
[3] Staedtler Triplus: https://amazon.com/dp/B009CQKL3Y
[4] Mattermost: https://about.mattermost.com

HipChat[5] is another chat option, but I do not like it. I say that as someone who uses it day-to-day. It loses notifications, the search stinks, and the interface just looks bland. Unless you have to use it, steer clear.

Slack also has an advantage when it comes to integrations. Many tools work with Slack out of the box through "bots" or small programs that listen and respond to text. HipChat has fewer, and from my experience, it is harder to write and integrate with.

I have not worked with Mattermost integrations myself, but they mention most of the popular tools and services people use and have an API. More information can be found at Mattermost Apps and Integrations[6].

When it comes to face-to-face—or rather voice-to-voice—communication, Hangouts is my recommendation. I have not found a cross-platform conferencing app that works as well. The video and audio clarity is pretty good, and screen sharing is one of the few that works cross-platform.

Skype's newer versions are shells of what the application used to be capable of, and the only cross-platform abilities are voice and video chat. Screen sharing only seems to work reliably if the sharer is on MacOS. If you just need voice or video chat, it works great, and for just a few dollars extra, you can do telephone calls. It is a decent replacement for a virtual phone for outgoing calls.

Calendars

I keep my calendar generally in sync with my notebook, since bullet journaling helps keep track of new events or events on a specific day. I usually copy information between my paper and Google calendar once a week.

While I am not a huge fan of Google knowing every little thing about me, I have not found a suitable replacement for Google Calendar. It works across all of my devices, which includes my phone, an iPad, my laptop, and my desktop running GNOME's Evolution email client. My day job uses GSuite for everything, so my work calendar gets synced as well.

Everything goes into the calendar, separated just by personal versus work calendars. The most obvious things, like appointments, travel, etc., go in, but anything that takes blocks of time does as well. If I want a block of time just to myself, I put it on the calendar. This practice is valuable when you need time to focus and review code or think about how to implement a requested feature. I love to watch motorsport racing, so on the days there are races I want to watch, I block those times out in my calendar.

You do have to make sure you respect these blocks of time. It is too easy to slip into the "well, I guess I'm not *really* busy during this time" guilt when someone asks you for a meeting or appointment that conflicts with your personal time. Making sure you have personal time, and respecting that time, is a great way to avoid burnout.

---

[5]   HipChat: https://www.hipchat.com
[6]   Mattermost Apps and Integrations: https://about.mattermost.com/?p=5761

4. Project Management Toolbox

At work, we also keep a shared calendar. It has all of our meetings and travel schedules. Making this information visible stops miscommunication when it comes to deadlines.

Speaking of deadlines, these go onto the calendar—preferably a shared one everyone can access. I mark down the end of our sprints, which are typically two months long, when the retrospective meetings should be, and when we should schedule releases.

For actually managing the calendar, I use a combination of the built-in iOS calendar application for my iPad, the Google Calendar application on my Android phone, Evolution on my desktop, and the web interface on my laptop. How well this data syncs and works across everything is a testament to open standards.

All of these apps—barring the website which I just use notifications with—all integrate with the host OS to show meeting notifications natively. This is a reason I do not recommend Thunderbird, which, while open-source, just does not work as well. It is also no longer maintained, so I doubt it will be around much longer.

> As of January 2020, Thunderbird[7] operates as a subsidiary of the Mozilla foundation, which should reinvigorate its development.

All that being said, if your job has specific software you need to use, find the best way to use it. It has been a while since I have used Outlook, but if that is what your company uses, find a way to make it work for you.

Tracking Projects

Most companies I have worked with do not have a very rigid organization structure when it comes to tracking issues that need to be worked on. If your company already has a workflow, by all means, use it. I do not recommend rocking the boat (unless the current workflow is not that great).

I like to use Kanban[8] as a project management system. When it comes to software development, Kanban is merely having a list of tasks that need to be done and picking what to work on from that list. For an excellent example of how it works, I highly recommend reading The Phoenix Project[9]. It does a good job of explaining the process and how it can help.

For basic projects, I put all the issues in a "Backlog" list or column. Then, I create a "Working" column to denote everything being worked on. As we complete issues, they go into a "Done" column for review. The issue can be looked at and then either merged or closed, and removed from the board or moved back to "Working."

---

[7] Thunderbird: https://blog.thunderbird.net/2020/01/thunderbirds-new-home/
[8] Kanban: https://en.wikipedia.org/wiki/Kanban
[9] The Phoenix Project: https://amazon.com/dp/B00AZRBLHO

I find this scales well. For more complex projects, I create a board for each major milestone or sprint and just fill the backlog with whatever the current smaller list needs. Another project can keep the main project backlog.

The key is letting developers find what to work on quickly, while also providing a good overview of the work and what still needs to be done for project owners. I can quickly show my bosses what work is being done and is still pending without looking at a massive list of issues.

If you use GitHub or GitHub Enterprise, you can do Kanban with the Project system. In each repository, there is a Projects tab. Under this tab, you can set up individual projects, and under each project, you can set up a series of columns. GitLab has a similar concept called "Issue Boards."

If you are not using Git, or just are not using one of the above systems, there is also Trello[10]. It allows you to create boards and projects and share them with others. There is a free tier, with the paid versions offering additional features.

Staying Organized Is Not Hard

I hope these tools and tips help keep you organized. Whether or not you want to use physical things like pen and paper, or you want to keep everything digital, the real key is just learning to keep track of things and finding tools that work for you. Keep what you can visible to all your team members, and keep everyone in the loop.

---

[10] Trello: https://trello.com

Chapter 5

Simple Project Management

One of the hardest things I have had to do as a developer is figuring out what in the world I am supposed to be doing on projects. I do not mean from a code standpoint, like what framework I should be using, or even an architectural viewpoint like what technologies I should be using. I'm talking about sitting down at my desk and determining what I should be doing today to get to my goal of having a finished product.

Methodologies

There are many different ways to figure this out in project management. They all boil down to the same thing, but you do the steps and processes in different orders or different periods. Some work well for some people, and some do not mesh with how some people work. I have stressed quite a bit about talking with people in this column, and ultimately you want to discuss with your team what works and what doesn't.

From a ten thousand foot view, you have two main types of project management. Generally considered older, and arguably the more hated, are non-iterative approaches. Non-iterative project

5. Simple Project Management

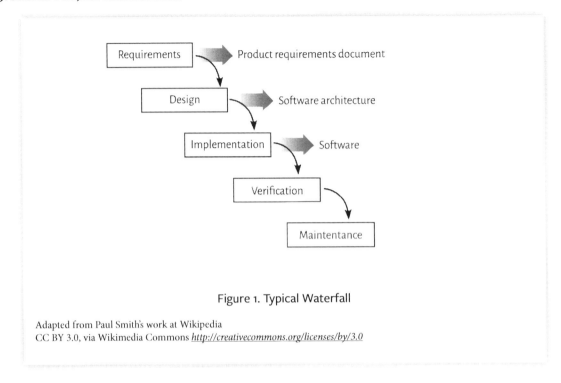

Figure 1. Typical Waterfall

Adapted from Paul Smith's work at Wikipedia
CC BY 3.0, via Wikimedia Commons http://creativecommons.org/licenses/by/3.0

management approaches are things like the Waterfall Method[1], or Big Design Up Front[2] (BDUF). In both cases, a significant amount of time is spent in the design and planning stages of a project before moving on to actual implementations. This approach worked well back in the early days of computing, such as the time Fred Brooks talks about in *The Mythical Man Month*[3]. It was incredibly expensive to build machines and hardware, and the software was often tailored to the device. Bugs in the hardware were more costly to fix compared to software.

The second type is iterative, or Agile[4], software development. Used much more frequently in "modern" workflows than non-iterative approaches, these types of processes are easy to jump into as they heavily promote coding and starting work right away. The design phase can be shortened, and the project can be tested much more quickly than in the past. Developers no longer need a comprehensive design statement to build software; they can take requirements directly to an implementation phase. If something does not work, it can quickly, and generally, cheaply, be changed or even thrown away.

[1] Waterfall Method: http://phpa.me/wikipedia-waterfall-model
[2] Big Design Up Front: http://phpa.me/wikipedia-bduf
[3] The Mythical Man Month: https://amazon.com/dp/0201835959
[4] Agile: http://phpa.me/wikipedia-agile-dev

While Agile is generally considered a newer method, both sets of software and project management have their roots in the late 1950s and early 60s of software development. Agile took a huge leap forward in the 1990s with movements like rapid application development, Unified Process, the Agile Manifesto, and even the popular Scrum. These processes fit well with the more "modern" way of doing software development.

In practice though, I find a healthy mixture of the two is needed. If you are having issues with your current project management and are looking for something different to try, read on. I have used this project management structure at multiple jobs and find, if nothing else, it is a good stepping stone into something that meshes well with your team.

Some Design Up Front

In a culture obsessed with shipping early (and before your competitors), very little time is spent on the design of a system. The goal of any startup is to get a prototype or a Minimum Viable Product (MVP) up and running as quickly as possible. It makes some sense; if your idea is not going to work, why spend a considerable amount of time or resources on developing sophisticated software? Developers and servers are expensive. Agile processes shine here.

Don't take technology choices lightly, and choosing a hosting platform or database backend is something to discuss and debate before implementation. There is nothing worse than being stuck with a technology or stack because "that's what was used in the MVP," or getting a pull request that is now dependent on a specific caching layer no one knew was coming.

At some point, someone has to decide how to build a fully working system. Since everyone throws away their prototypes like they are supposed to (if you are not, you did not make a prototype—you built a product you now have to maintain), this is the perfect time to sit down and look at your application. What is it supposed to do? What did you find during your MVP stage that you need to change? If given infinite money and infinite developer time, what constitutes the perfect version of this application?

Write all of these things down on cards. It doesn't matter if they are on physical index cards or post-it notes, in a GitHub project board, or in a Trello board. Write all of them down. **All of them.** No idea is too outlandish at this stage. Talk to product owners, other developers, actual users; find out their wants, their dreams, and their complaints.

Then, go through the list with everyone involved. At this point, you start to design your software. Unfortunately, you do not have infinite money or infinite developer time. Some of the user complaints will be invalid, and some of the things you want do not make sense in the grand scheme of things. Go ahead and weed out these things.

Don't just say, "Yeah, this sounds good," and move on. Think about each feature in the context of the entire system. Will it work? How hard will it be to implement? Start thinking about the technologies you will need to use, or services you will be dependent on. These considerations are all part of the design phase.

5. Simple Project Management

Define your users. Some developers find it a waste of time, but coming up with users and their personas help steer feature designs. If it is an older crowd, they interact with websites and applications differently than a younger group. Are your users computer savvy in general, or are you targeting someone who only knows how to turn on a PC and use the internet? How will they use your application? Are there bandwidth considerations? Many rural customers are on slow broadband and could be aggravated by a large page download. This connectivity can limit the types of features you want to provide to a user.

A relevant example of this is when I worked for a company that dealt with Google Ads. We had a giant list of great ideas and features to make it easier to work with Google Ads. But, some features did not make sense at all for the companies we were selling to. If you are targeting small to mid-size businesses, features which target millions of ads are very different from features that work with a handful of ads. Conversely, dealing with millions of ads requires an entirely different interface than handling campaigns with ten or so ads.

Many project managers love Agile because you can just throw everything into a pot, but it's not that simple. Some technologies do not work well with others or provide additional challenges. Some features are just not feasible starting out. Now is the time to figure that out.

Stealing a term from Agile, we will call that big list of items we have the *backlog*. This list will grow and shrink over time.

Scheduling

Coming up with features is easy. Scheduling is hard. What makes something more important than something else? Why should something get done before something else? These are questions all your development chops cannot answer.

Someone will have to, however. Now is also the time to start to think about release schedules. Are you going to be doing something like continuous deployment, constantly rolling out new features to customers? Are you doing bi-weekly or monthly releases? Quarterly? Start to answer these questions now.

I have done all sorts of release schedules, but the release schedule needs to make sense for your team and your product. If you are building a SaaS platform, you can probably do daily or weekly releases. If you are developing software someone is installing, you need to release often, but not so frequently that your customers/users get nagging notifications to update. You do not want to wait so long between releases serious issues linger.

I like a two-week development cycle, followed by one week of testing. If you have a dedicated QA department, they can test as changes are made, but very few places seem to have dedicated testing teams. At my current job, we do major releases quarterly and usually monthly bugfix releases. This cadence works well for the software we sell and for our customers.

Take a look at that backlog you have. Start to order things by importance. Which of the items in the backlog are the most important? These can be customer requests, developer requests, infrastructure requests, anything you need to do to build your application. Order and rank them.

Then look at your release schedule. Let's assume a two-week development and one-week testing cycle. Starting from the top of your list, what can you do in two weeks? Estimation is a wonderfully inexact science, so use your best guess. You will be wrong on some items. That is okay.

Most importantly, *push back*. If someone wants a feature that takes too long or requires something else, which then makes the feature implementation take longer than your release schedule, *push back*. It is okay to say no. If something is paramount for a release, do not be afraid to speak up and request something else slip, or be removed from the scheduled items. Alternatively, if the estimation for something is multi-weeks or multi-days, see if the task can be broken down. You might end up finding out the feature is not so important.

Communication during scheduling is one of the most important things you can do correctly. Your team relies on you to help make sure they have enough work, but not an overwhelming amount. Do not lie about how much *can* get done, but do not put things on the schedule that *cannot* be done in time. Burn out and loss of productivity from long hours is real. Again, you will make some mistakes, but estimation can be hard. That is very different from scheduling a three-week development feature in two weeks of space.

The items we are picking for the release will be our release issues. If you have done Agile before, this will be very familiar as a sprint backlog.

Stick It on a Board

Once you have decided on your items for the two weeks, put it on a board. I usually have four columns, like in Figure 2.

- **Release Issues**, which are everything we are working on for a release.
- **Working**, for issues actively being worked on by a developer.
- **QA**, for anything in testing.
- **Done**, for anything which is finished.

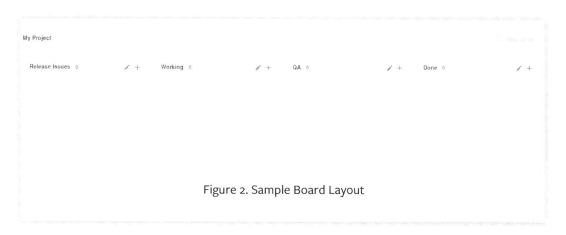

Figure 2. Sample Board Layout

5. Simple Project Management

All of the items you selected for your two-week development schedule go into Release Issues. They then move from there to Working when someone starts to work on it. When completed, it goes into QA for testing. Once it has been tested properly, it moves to Done.

If you are using GitHub, create individual milestones for each release and set the due date to the end of the development period. Doing so allows me not only to visualize where a single issue is—not worked one, working, QA, etc.—but also an overall view of how far along we are in a release. If we are not roughly 50% finished by the end of the first week, we find out why. This view is especially helpful on longer release cycles and can be a better indicator for other teams and management on how far along a release is.

I don't worry about things like burndown charts, or velocity, or anything like them. I find they are not a good indicator of how far along a process is since individual items can be flexible in their time. As you and your team work together more, you can estimate more accurately, and catch potential slowdowns along the way.

Keep in constant communication with your team during the development time. I look at the board every morning and assess where we are. I generally do not do standup meetings every day like Scrum recommends, as I find them mostly useless in a functional team. Your team should not be waiting until a meeting is happening to mention hangups, or request help from someone else, or to update the board. I should be able to see the status of an item in real time, and teammates should be able to communicate day-to-day on issues. If they cannot, find out why.

Quick status updates at the beginning of the week work just as well. I keep this meeting to under one hour, usually trying to hit no more than thirty minutes. Why? I can see where issues are at on the board, and I follow the discussions. I talk to my team. Constant meetings cause interruptions which can be hard to come back from, especially with distributed teams when finding times that work for everyone can be hard. So while I do not hover over my team micro-managing, I keep tabs on them through the project board.

One other important note about the board is that only issues slated for the release go on the board. This rule helps funnel everyone to work on the items deemed important. If something else comes up, you can make a distinction as to whether or not it goes into the board, or into the backlog.

Most of this workflow is taken from Kanban[5], which is based on lean manufacturing techniques inspired by the Toyota Production System, and workflows developed at Microsoft. The overarching idea is to work from a bucket of ideas, in any order, and keep track of them throughout the process. The Phoenix Project[6] is an excellent read which shows some of this in action.

---

[5] Kanban: http://phpa.me/wikipedia-kanban
[6] The Phoenix Project: https://amazon.com/dp/B00AZRBLHO

The Retrospective and Restart the Cycle

Once your two weeks are up and you have gone through your testing, release your code. Enjoy the fruits of your labor. Then go back to your backlog. Discuss what is most important. Put it in a new release, and start the cycle over again. During this time also talk about issues we encountered with the release. Is a technology not working? Was something hard to implement? Did we get stuck waiting for something? The retrospective is not a time to blame anyone, but a time to reflect and discover pain points. Once we know where there are issues, we can start to solve them.

After your release, look to the backlog and see if there is anything new that you can add. You can add to the backlog at any time. If new features are deemed important compared to before, this is a good time to sit down, have a discussion, and plan going forward. I never advocate pivoting during the middle of a release, and fight hard against scope creep, but starting a new version means anything is fair game.

After your team retrospective, take the lessons learned to the other teams and management. Let them know how things went, what could be done better, and what worked well. Have opinions on what the next steps should be.

Simple Project Management for an Easier Workday

All of this helps not only with making development go smoothly but also helps keep unnecessary features in check. The up-front time spent on the backlog helps focus on and sketch out the broad strokes of the application. The individual talks leading up to each release timeline help reinforce that the most important and fruitful ideas are being worked on.

Keeping up on issues helps identify scope creep. When issues are not moving along the board in a reasonable amount of time, you can catch them before it becomes a huge issue. Do not be afraid to say no, but do not be afraid to compromise either. Work with your team to make sure goals are being met, and everyone has everything they need.

Hopefully, this helps you a bit when it comes to project management. Adapt the above to whatever works for your team, or if none of this sounds that great, wonderful! I have at least helped you identify workflows you don't think will work for your team.

Chapter 6

How Long Will It Take?

Let's discuss what we can do to help come up with better estimates. I hate estimating, but it is an unfortunate part of software development. We cannot come up with schedules without estimates. My boss wants to know I'm not wasting his time when I say something will take 40 developer hours. I want to make sure my team is doing things in the best possible order and not waiting until the very end to deliver a big feature.

There are plenty of different ways to come up with estimates, and I want to run you through my thoughts, workflows, and tools for how I estimate issues. I cannot make you get exact estimations, but I can hopefully make you feel more confident in the estimations you make.

Estimates are only estimates.

For this chapter, we should look at a seemingly simple yet complex issue—let's add token authentication to our legacy application with the following user story:

"As a consumer of our API, I can access endpoints without having to use a stateful client that relies on cookies and sessions."

6. How Long Will It Take?

Divide and Conquer

If I gave you the above user story, I apologize. It has all of the markings of a user story that is a pain to work on. It is incredibly vague and does not provide any information on what needs to happen to implement this user story. Read the relevant chapters to learn how to provide details and to flesh out an issue to make sure developers get the information they need.

This user story does show that a simple request—adding an API token to requests—can have some substantial hidden challenges. At the beginning of estimating an issue, developers are faced with their first obstacle, the Cone of Uncertainty[1].

The Cone of Uncertainty explains that developers start with the largest amount of risk and uncertainty with a project. This situation only gets worse if goals are shifting or stakeholders are frequently changing their minds. The only way to decrease the cone is to conduct research and development.

Broader issues increase the amount of uncertainty a developer will face. As you start to touch more pieces of the software, such as authentication, UI, UX, database schemas, etc., the uncertainty of changes rises. It can cause a developer to pad or inflate the estimate.

If I handed you the above user story, you should have a bunch of questions. How are we generating the token? Is this a token used in something like an HMAC authentication scheme or just a simple API token? Is the client restricted to just passing it through query parameters, or can they pass it via HTTP request headers? Have you ever built anything like this before to even gauge the amount of work?

There is a tremendous amount of uncertainty in our user story. The first thing to do is break down the issue into the smallest possible chunks of work; then we can estimate those individually. This process is formally called creating a work breakdown structure[2]. You list out all of the features or work required to satisfy 100 percent of the issue.

Without having to waste much of your time, we can break this down into the following chunks:

1. System generated tokens
2. Linking tokens to users
3. Authentication based on token
4. Stateless API endpoints

We still have some overall architectural questions, like query parameter token versus HMAC in the header, key length, etc.. Nevertheless, we can start to tackle the above in more manageable pieces. I am leaving out time costs like QA, testing, documentation, and focusing on development tasks, and I will discuss these later.

We can estimate how long it will take to add a token to the user objects and display it on a page. We can estimate how long it will take to add key generation. We can estimate how long it will take to audit the endpoints.

[1] Cone of Uncertainty: https://phpa.me/wikip-cone-uncertainty
[2] work breakdown structure: https://phpa.me/wikip-work-breakdown

One rule of thumb I try to stick to is any individual chunk should not take more than eight developer hours to work on. If it takes more than a single workday to finish, it can be broken down into smaller chunks.

Queueing theory[3] also suggests breaking things down into smaller, more manageable chunks, and being able to parallelize workflows can lead to an increase in throughput. If we estimate that each issue above takes four developer hours each, we can look at breaking up who does work. We should also keep in mind Brook's Law from "The Mythical Man Month," which states that adding people to a project can increase the amount of time a project takes. It becomes a balancing act between bringing people into an issue without causing much in the way of impediments.

We might be able to see that tasks one and two should be worked on by the same person, but three and four can be worked on by others. We can have the work split between three developers instead of one. You may not be able to break things up between developers this way, and it does not change the overall total estimate, but it can help some issues be delivered faster.

We then just total all of that up, and we can create a rough estimate.

Lies...I Mean Numbers

Once we have broken an issue down into its parts, we can start to figure out how long these parts will take. There are many different ways to come up with estimates. These are generally divided into three different techniques:

- Expert Estimation: Estimates are determined on a judgemental basis by a person.
- Formal Estimation: Mathematical formulas derived from historical data.
- Combination-based Estimation: A combination of the above two types.

Expert Estimation is rather simple—just lie. Okay, I'm not suggesting this, but hey, it's an option! If different theories have similar accuracy when all else fails—just come up with a number.

For something a bit more serious, your gut is a good indicator. Being able to trust your instincts is not just a lie, as it should come with a good dose of experience. I would take the gut estimate of a senior developer over a junior developer due to the senior developer's breadth of knowledge and comfort with the system they work in. For all of the fancy systems I've used, experience tends to be a good indicator for estimates.

Once you've implemented authentication systems two or three times, you start to develop the know-how to implement it the fourth time. You know some of the pitfalls you can run into. You also know some of the questions you should ask. It is horribly unscientific, but many estimation techniques rely on expert knowledge. Do not sell yourself short.

If you take the breakdown we created above using the Work Breakdown Structure, you can simply estimate each section based on judgment and total everything up. There are also options like

---

[3]   Queueing theory: https://phpa.me/wikip-queue-theory

6. How Long Will It Take?

planning poker[4] or Wideband Delphi[5] which take into account multiple people estimating a unit of work until they reach consensus. The advantage of group estimation is the discussion surrounding the estimates as these can uncover new techniques and pitfalls of design.

One of the more popular (or hated) methods of Formal Estimation is story points, or Use Case Points[6]. This method assigns points to the relative complexity of a task, where more complex tasks cost more points. The idea is that a more complex task should take longer than a simple task. From there, you can somewhat derive a developer-hour amount, though story points are not meant to substitute for hours directly. For further discussion, see Story Points vs. Hours[7].

I like using story points when trying to weigh out the amount of work, but not necessarily for the duration of work. In the end, most higher-ups do not care about the complexity; they want to know the time. I do feel more comfortable giving a quick estimate on a simple issue versus a more complex one. In the end, though, it all comes back to developer hours.

Your Estimates Are Wrong

And they always will be. I do not like writing out an article with a defeatist attitude, but indulge me for just a moment longer before you abandon this article and move onto something else.

Estimates are nothing more than guesses. As developers, we sail on ships battered by uncertainty. We have to deal with half-baked requirements, continually shifting priorities, and technical debt we cannot even begin to imagine. We start the estimation process at such a disadvantage it is not funny.

That does not mean we should not try our hardest to come up with an estimate for work, but we should remember we are providing nothing more than an educated guess. Estimates are useful for scheduling and deciding between what goes into a release, and when.

One thing most developers hate is someone saying, "Oh, this shouldn't take long." It invalidates the expertise at which we do our jobs and makes developers feel bad when they can't meet someone else's estimate. Imposter syndrome can easily set in. On the other end, developers may feel they are being ignored, and this can lead to anger.

Estimates are only valid for the person coming up with an estimate. There are plenty of times where I think a task is relatively trivial, but it turns out it takes two or three times as long to implement. As a lead developer, I may weigh in on estimations when deciding when to put on the schedule, but the real estimation lies on who is assigned to the work.

None of this has to do with the ability of the developer. There are things I am quicker at than others, and there are tasks others are faster at than myself. There are also plenty of circumstances which may cause an unanticipated hangup.

[4] planning poker: https://phpa.me/wikip-planning-poker
[5] Wideband Delphi: https://phpa.me/wikip-wideband-delphi
[6] Use Case Points: https://phpa.me/wikip-use-case-points
[7] Story Points vs. Hours: https://phpa.me/rubygarage-story-points

When I am forced to estimate for someone else, I will try and get a rough estimate from whom I think will be doing the work.

Estimates are also highly tied to your situation at this moment. If I say something will take twelve hours to complete, the assumption is that I am estimating the work based on what the system looks like today.

Estimates Are Not Deadlines

One final, quick addition to all of this is that estimates are not, and should not be considered deadlines. This will probably be one of the largest fights you as a lead developer will have to make, but you will need to make other teams and your managers understand that estimates are guidelines, not deadlines.

If my team decides an issue is going to take 40 developer hours, that does not mean we will be delivering it to the customer in 40 developer hours. Many other factors come into play when it comes to deliverables. End-user documentation, training, packaging, user acceptance, installation, scheduling downtime, etc., these are all things that impact deliverable time.

I feel like this is where people get hung up on "take your estimates and multiply it by four." There are so many other things that go into finishing a project outside of the estimate. When estimates are used as deadlines, we fall into traps.

Estimates Are Important

In the end, estimates are one of the most critical parts of a software development lifecycle, as they allow us to make decisions on what goes into a project. If I have only two months to deliver a new release, I need to know how many features I can plan. If I am working around deploying based on features, how long will the new requests take?

Estimates are the scariest thing a developer can do because of the uncertainty. I say embrace it and follow your gut. If you have made it to a lead developer position, it is because you have shown your expertise in software development. You are being paid to make good decisions. Part of that comes in the form of knowing how hard or how long something will take.

Ultimately, developers know estimates are based on lies we tell ourselves, but with some planning, we can overcome that. Embrace the lie and believe in yourself and your team.

Chapter 7

Issue Workflows for Teams

Issues and issue tracking are central to your team's communications about what's getting worked on and needs fixing. Having a clear and agreed-upon standard for working with them will keep your team focused and productive while minimizing misunderstanding.

For the sake of this chapter, we will work with a sample issue. Our example application is a basic note-taking application where the user logs in, sees a list of notes, and can add, create, or delete them (if you would like to help finance this fresh startup idea of mine, please e-mail me). When working with the application, our tester found a bug where save validation would cause the user interface to switch from Markdown to HTML entities, which messed up the writing—`## My Heading` became `&num;&num; My Heading`.

We will walk through the process of creating an issue, fixing the code, and getting it into production. I will be using Git and GitHub as the primary vehicle for this exercise, but you can use whatever source control mechanism or tools you want.

7. Issue Workflows for Teams

Create an Issue

Once someone discovers a problem or even has a new feature, it needs to be documented as an issue. I will not accept any pull request without an issue attached. No one should be working on pull requests without one in the first place, because issues are the first line of defense from a project management standpoint. They are used to drive sprints and work.

Issues should have a consistent look and feel, and each should have enough information that any developer can pick it up and work on it. I hate having issues with just one or two lines of information. Each one should have at least the following information:

1. description
2. expected behavior
3. actual behavior
4. possible fix
5. steps to reproduce
6. context
7. environment

Description

The "Description" section should be a general overview of what the issue itself is. We flesh out the problem in the other sections, but here we can give a tl;dr. I use this to catch up quickly on new issues that are not specific to my team. Do not feel the need to be heavily detailed here.

> *When saving a note which fails validation, the note is returned as HTML entities instead of the original text.*

Expected Behavior

"Expected Behavior" is what you wanted to happen. In our case, we expected validation to fail and get a pop-up indicating the validation failed. If you can, point to documentation explaining how something should work, especially if this was existing behavior. If this is in regards to new behavior (for example, a new feature), you may want to note you are expecting production behavior versus new feature behavior, if it is known.

> *Clicking "Save Note" should have popped up an error saying that the note could not be saved, with an appropriate explanation. I could then correct the problem and save the note.*

Actual Behavior

"Actual Behavior" is what really happened. You want to have as much information here as possible about the error, but we detail how to cause the error later.

> *Clicking "Save Note" popped up an error saying the note could not be saved, with an appropriate explanation. In this case, it said that the title contained invalid characters. It then turned the note text into HTML-escaped entities, so all of my # signs became #, ! became !, etc. While I could correct the title and save the note, I lost all the formatting because of this.*

Possible Fix

"Possible Fix" is helpful for future you, if you are going to be the one to fix this or another developer *if you have something constructive to add*. I like to leave this for comments where you have an understanding of the issue and can provide a possible fix. Do not make assumptions about what the problem is unless you have dug into it. I would rather see "N/A" here than guesses as to a fix.

> *Move the* `htmlentities()` *call from* `App\Notes\Note::setNoteText()` *to* `App\Notes\Repository::save()`, *after validation, to avoid escaping this data too early in the process.*

Steps to Reproduce

Now we can detail how to reproduce the issue under "Steps to Reproduce." Detail what you did to cause the error, and be specific. Do not say something like, "Put in a title with invalid characters," as maybe it is an issue with a particular validation which fails. You want the eventual developer to follow in your exact footsteps.

> 1. *Create a new note.*
> 2. *Add "**SUPER COOL TITLE!!!!@!" as the title.*
> 3. *Enter "## My title" as the note text.*
> 4. *Save the note.*

Context

"Context" is essential from a project management standpoint. This part is where you explain why something is important and how it affected you as a user. If it is a minor bug with a workaround or is in a lightly used portion of the system, I might skip this for a bit before working on it. Explain how this affects your usage of the system, and kind of "sell" the issue a bit.

7. Issue Workflows for Teams

> *This makes it very hard to work on notes, as a simple title validation completely messes up the text. If this was a long note, it could potentially cause a user to spend a tremendous amount of time reformatting text for something as simple as a single-character fix with the title.*

Environment

Finally, we have "Environment." How you need to fill this out will depend on your application. At my job, we require a browser, environment (production, testing, local), and the version of our application. If you have a SaaS product, you can probably get away with the browser and what environment. You want to be able to determine if this is a production-level issue affecting customers or just something someone came across during testing.

> *Browser: Google Chrome*
>
> *Environment: production*

Feel free to use the above to create an issue template, or use something like *Open Source Templates*[1] to come up with one.

One thing the user does not necessarily do at this stage is to assign issue labels if you are using something like GitHub. I reserve this for triage. It can be useful to have a "Triage Needed" label to make it easier to find, but I do not usually let the issue author label things.

Triage

When someone finds a new bug, their first instinct is to get it fixed. It is a bug, and bugs affect software, and therefore they all need to be fixed. Reality is a bit more nuanced because software also has deadlines. Deadlines were agreed upon before this bug was discovered, so now we need to do a bit of project management.

This one can be tricky because this bug might not get fixed right away. When a new issue comes in, it should not necessarily be worked on right away as something else might be more critical. In medical terms, we need to "triage" the issue to determine how serious it is, how much time we think it will take, and how imperative it is to address.

Triaging an issue does not mean figuring out a fix, but simply figuring out how severe something is. When you go into the emergency room, a nurse might ask you things like, "Are you having trouble breathing?", "Can you walk under your own power?", or "Did you hit your head when you fell?" If you answer "No," "Yes," and "No," they might decide to let the person who cannot breathe go before you.

The same is true with issues. In the case of our ticket, we have a problem affecting users in production and has the potential to make a bunch of users mad. We should make this a pretty high priority.

---

[1] Open Source Templates: https://phpa.me/open-source-templates

I can make this assumption based on the information in the issue itself, under "Context," "Environment," and "Actual Behavior." I do not need to go back to the issue author to get more information.

In the case of GitHub, I would label this as "bug," high priority," and "customer impacting." I can now find it more easily when looking for serious things to work on right away for sprints and can make sure that this does not get lost in the shuffle as we plan new sprints.

Sprint Planning

Sprint planning covers both the initial planning of a sprint as well as ongoing grooming of the sprint while it is active. For those of you not familiar with the term sprint, it is a term from the Agile development movement, which defines a span of time and the work to be done during that time. Typical sprints are two to three weeks, and at the end of it, you should have deployable code.

Sprint planning happens right before starting a sprint. It is when you review your issues and decide what you need to work on this sprint. In my case, each sprint begins with going through the issues labeled "bug," "high priority," or "customer impacting." For me, those are things that should be looked at immediately, especially if multiple labels appear on the same issue.

I then move onto the features we need. "Customer request" is a label we use to determine things customers have asked for but are generally new features. We also have an internal roadmap of priorities and features, so this list is also consulted. People can make a case for specific things, but ultimately you pick a handful of issues you think can be completed in time and match your roadmap.

If issues come up in the middle of a sprint, like this bug, it is up to the project managers to decide if the issue gets put into a sprint. Never assume a bug is okay to add and work on—that is not a developer's decision to make, it is the project manager's decision. This rule sounds pretty authoritarian, but again, the sprint was built around a specific deadline with specific issues. New issues can mess up the timetable.

In our case, this is a pretty serious issue. We should work on it right away, and the project manager agrees.

Since this has the potential to mess up the deadline, the project manager can consult with the team to determine if it will. If it does, something else must slip to make room. This change can be a team decision, but especially managers and higher-ups should be consulted. Slipping something on your team might impact another team, so keep communication open and transparent.

If you read the chapter on *Simple Project Management*, we will add the issue to the "Release Issues" board in Github, and assign it to a developer.

Working an Issue

Now comes our favorite part—development. With a well-written issue, the developer should have enough information to get started on the feature.

7. Issue Workflows for Teams

I like the GitFlow[2] workflow, so we use it internally at my day job; while we do have a web interface for our software, we operate more like a traditional software development house and have structured application releases. If you are doing more daily releases to something like a SaaS, GitHub Flow[3] may make more sense.

In either case, the developer should make a new branch off of whatever is the appropriate base branch. At work, this would be off of our "develop" branch, but for you, it might be "master." The key idea is that the developer will be working in their branch for the life of this issue.

The developer can work on the issue locally as much as they want, but eventually, they will need to push the branch up somewhere to have a pull request generated. On internal projects, we handle branches all in the central repository, but developers can work on their forks. If this is an open-source project, or you want to keep the main repository cleaner, you can have each developer work in their fork, and push branches to their fork. It is technically cleaner, but I find most tools work better when branches are all in the same repository.

In any event, the branch gets pushed up, and a pull request is created against the base branch so it can be reviewed. Each pull request should have the following information:

1. description
2. related issues
3. motivation and context
4. How has this been tested?
5. screenshots
6. types of changes

Description

"Description" is like the issue itself but focused on the work you did, rather than the bug itself. Give a brief description of what work you did to fix the issue. You can be more descriptive here than on the issue itself because there are no other sections to expand upon what you did.

> *Fixed an issue where validation would cause the* `App\Notes\Notes` *object to return HTML escaped text. This was due to text sanitization happening at save time instead of display time and was causing display issues not only when saving but also displaying information to non-HTML displays. HTML sanitization has been moved to the view layer.*

---

[2]   GitFlow: *https://phpa.me/intro-gitflow*
[3]   GitHub Flow: *https://phpa.me/github-flow*

Related Issues

"Related Issues" should list all of the issues this pull request covers. At the very least, it should be the single issue which spawned the fix but can also encompass multiple issues if warranted. If you are using GitHub, you can use text like "Resolves #X" to work with issue automation. A reviewer should be able to determine what issues this PR covers.

> *Resolves #128, #157*

Motivation and Context

"Motivation and Context" handle the why of the change, and why you picked the current solution. It may be as simple as it was the fix, but you can expand upon your development decision here if there were competing solutions. This explanation helps the reviewer get into your mindset, and can help answer questions they might have about why you did something a specific way.

> *Originally, the application was built as a web-only system. Since then, we have added a desktop application, mobile app, and various export functions. When everything was web-only, we could get away with making everything just HTML entities, but now that we are working with multiple formats, we should let the format decide. As such, we now handle visual sanitization in the various* `App\Export\*` *classes.*

How Has This Been Tested?

As a good developer, one should detail how this has been tested under "How Has This Been Tested?" Explain what you as the developer did to test, so the reviewer can do the same thing. Here is where unit and integration tests shine; you can point to the new tests as validation.

> *Created a new note with the original bad title, saved it, and checked the output. Also viewed another issue in the web app, and exported it as both HTML and plaintext to check formatting. [Zip file is attached]*

Screenshots and Types of Changes

"Screenshots" can help further show how something changed.

"Types of Changes" is a simple checklist of whether something is a bug fix, new feature, or a breaking change. These categories help with project management and planning when to merge something.

Reviewing the PR

With all of this information, the pull request can be effectively reviewed. The reviewer gains a better understanding of the original issue, how it was fixed, and how to test it. The hope is the reviewer can have less back-and-forth by having all of this information up front.

The March 2018 issue of php[architect] details setting up, enforcing, and performing the actual code review. *Open Source Templates*[4] is a great place to help work on your templates if you want to use something other than what I recommend above.

Completing the Merge

Once we accept the pull request, all that is left is to merge it. It can be done right away, or at the end of a sprint if need be. I usually merge all pull requests as soon as they are tested and reviewed, but that is because we do not deploy right away. The merged issues sit until we do a full release.

Whatever time you merge it, the original issue can then be closed. I try and let the original author close it, but honestly, at this point, we have a well-formed issue body, a PR that has been reviewed and tested, and a sufficient amount of confidence the issue has been fixed.

Once the issue is merged, it's lifecycle is complete.

The hardest part of this lifecycle is enforcement. GitHub allows for creating templates to help with this, though we have found issues where command-line tools that generate issues or PRs completely ignore templates. The code review process helps make sure new issues are effectively fixed.

I hope this helps shed light on a good workflow for you and your coworkers. It puts together some of the code review elements I talked about in March 2018, as well as the Simple Project Management tips in the November 2017 issue. While I did use git and GitHub, these overall ideas can easily be used in just about any system. Good luck!

---

[4] *Open Source Templates:* https://phpa.me/open-source-templates

Chapter 8

From Issues to Code

In the *Issue Workflows for Teams* chapter, I talked about establishing a workflow to handle the issues your team will be working on. Everyone on your team should have a good idea of the actual problem or feature they are working on before writing any code. Once the issue itself is ready to go, the work can begin.

Every company will be slightly different in how they want to handle actual commits, but this month I will detail the most common workflows I use with teams. As with most of my advice, you can adapt it to your situation. Any changes you make to this—or even with integrating into your existing workflows—should be done with consideration for your team's productivity.

Origin, Upstream, and Forks

Before I get into the nitty-gritty about repository structure and workflow, I want to go ahead and cover how you handle forks and such out of the way.

It ultimately doesn't matter, but I suggest a centralized setup where everyone is pushing and pulling to the same repository. All branches live in the central repository, and all pull requests come from branches on the central repository. I find it useless in a corporate structure to make pull requests come from external forks.

8. From Issues to Code

Yes, this is a hill I will probably die on, but this is my column, so it is my advice. Having a centralized repository does not stop you from having a fork of a project, but modern source control software allows administrators to control who has access to what branch. It also dramatically simplifies keeping branches up-to-date as there is no more pulling from upstreaming, hard resetting, and force-pushing to local forks.

If you want to have your local repository or a fork in your corporate GitHub or GitLab, go ahead. I would strongly suggest enforcing a rule that all PRs and finished branches *must* go to the central repository. I would also enforce some shared verbiage to keep everyone on the same page:

- `upstream`—the central repository
- `origin`—your local fork

Never directly modify any branches that are not yours, and keep them in sync with the upstream repository as much as possible. This practice will avoid conflicts.

Keep in mind this is a recommendation for a corporate project, not an open-source library. Open source structures rely on the idea of forks, and I would never suggest opening up public codebases directly to the world for commits.

From a Good Base

For the most part, I like to use gitflow[1] as the basis for a project's branching structure. This workflow works well if your project has a release schedule, or is installable by your users. If you are working on a software-as-a-service type product, or you are using Continuous Delivery, you can still use this setup but with some minor modifications.

The basis of this workflow is two main branches: `master` and `develop`. `master` is code that is released to your customers and contains all of the release tags. Release tags are tagged versions used for deployment. We will talk more about them later.

The `develop` branch is the code waiting to go out to customers. `develop` will continue to get new features up until the time you decide to release all the features to your customers. You decide when that happens, but `develop` will always be marching toward the next release.

When you are happy with `develop`, you will merge it into `master`, create a release tag, and then deliver it to your customer. That is the heart of gitflow, and other workflows like the "Git Branch Model." This differs from the GitHub Workflow where you have `master` as a base, which I find does not work well for full-on applications.

I like this model because it gives you the ability to track releases through the release tags, and stops `master` from getting polluted with potentially bad or broken code. At worst, `develop` may be broken for a short while but end-users and customers will never see that code. If you want to release code early to customers, you still can, but your main release code stays pristine.

---

[1] gitflow: https://phpa.me/atlassian-gitflow

If you do not have both of these branches, it is straightforward to switch to having a dedicated `master` and `develop` branch. It is as easy as:

```
git branch -b develop
```

Branching Out

When most people talk about gitflow or look up gitflow, they immediately see this massively complex graph of how branches work. I am not going to show you that graph because it is scary. It makes a fairly basic concept look complicated.

The first thing we need to do is look at our issue. Issues will come in three basic types:

1. **New Feature**: Brand new code for a brand new set of functionality.
2. **Bug**: A problem with existing code that is not an emergency.
3. **Hotfix**: A bug that needs to be corrected outside of your standard release cycle.

You may or may not have more labels than that, but ultimately we are making new things, fixing broken things that can be broken for a while, or fixing things right now—also known as putting out a fire. How and where we branch from depends on the issue.

New features and bugs should both branch from the `develop` branch. Both of these issue types can take their time being worked on as the idea is they can be pushed out with a release. You should be able to safely branch off of the latest `develop` and begin working.

I recommend naming the branch `issue/[issue#]-a-short-description` as the branch name. If we have Issue #301 to add a field to users named "Location," we might do this:

```
git checkout develop
git checkout -b issue/301-user-location-field
```

This naming convention is useful for several reasons. We know the leading `issue/` denotes this as a general issue. `301` tells us the issue number in our tracker, and `user-location-field` gives us a quick overview of the problem. I can quickly scan branches and tie them back to issue numbers and vice-versa.

If the issue is a hotfix, or something that must be released out of our release cycle—say, issue #199 where users cannot log in—we branch off of the `master` branch from the release tag we are fixing. Normally, this should be the latest release which is the current HEAD of `master` so we will create a new branch from there but with a slight change:

```
git checkout master
git checkout -b hotfix/199-user-logins-fail
```

It is the same idea, just with a bit of different naming. The prefix `hotfix/` tells me this is a hotfix, and I still have an issue number and description.

8. From Issues to Code

Working on Branches

Now that we have a branch, you can begin work! Write your tests, watch them fail, create code, and just all around do everything you can to fix that code. I don't care how, but do everything in your power to fix the issue.

My first suggestion is to put your issue number at the end of your commit summary. Doing so allows someone else to see what commit goes with what issue number. It may not be totally obvious why "Added missing avatar" was done, but "Added missing avatar (#457)" can let someone go back and reference an issue.

Once you are happy with your code, push the branch up to the repository (or `upstream`, if you are using forks), and create your pull request.

Squashing Commits

There is another hill I am going to climb, and this time it is in regards to squashing commits. You can take or leave this one, but hear me out; I have a good reason for suggesting this.

Every commit in Git should be a fully atomic commit. *Everything* should be a single commit, and if I need to remove a feature or a fix, all I need to do is remove a single commit. That single commit should contain your tests, your documentation (if your documentation is stored with your code), your fix, any database migrations, etc. This single issue should ultimately have a single commit.

When you are finished with your issue and are ready to submit a pull request, you should rebase and squash your commits into a single commit before creating the pull request. Take the following `git log` for example:

```
8dbfad7e6 (HEAD -> issue/301-user-location-field) Added user creation documentation
1b0dfee78 Added missing test for empty location field
4dedfaded Added location field to the user entity
26472c734 Added migration for location field
76ea1c190 (origin/develop, develop) Fixed State drop-down (#123)
```

We had four commits for our branch (26472c734, 4dedfaded, 1b0dfee78, and 8dbfad7e6). Since none of those satisfy our issue by themselves, we should squash them down to a single commit.

```
$ git rebase -i 76ea1c190
```

You can then elect to squash everything down into a single commit by marking everything after 26472c734 as squash, and rewording the final squashed commit appropriately, with the issue number.

This gives you the flexibility of being able to test and roll back commits locally, but then leaves a clean history when we go to merge it in. As a team lead, I do not care what steps you took to resolve the issue at such a fine-grained level; I care if you solved the problem. This is a decision for you to make with your team.

The only caveat is this works locally only, and if you are working on a branch with someone else, you should not be doing this. Squashing all of your commits down into a single one only works when you are the only one touching the branch. As soon as you hand it off to someone else for their commits, never rebase unless you have a good reason.

Rebasing on Newer develop

If your branch has lived for a long while, either due to a feature slipping or it just taking a while for an issue to get resolved, you will slowly diverge from the underlying `develop` branch.

When this happens, I recommend rebasing on `develop` rather than merging `develop` back into your branch. This generally leads to a cleaner, more linear commit history. I prefer that to a mess of branching/merging/changes/merging in my history.

If you are working with other people on a branch that needs rebasing, just make sure you tell the others before you rebase. They will need to re-pull the branch and hard reset to get synced back up properly.

The Pull Request

In _Chapter 7_, I mentioned that a pull request should contain the following information:

- **Description:** Quick overview of what you did.
- **Related Issues:** The issue(s) this branch is meant to resolve.
- **Motivation and Context:** Why you did the fix the way you did.
- **How Has This Been Tested?** How you tested it.
- **Screenshots:** Relevant screenshots.
- **Types of Changes:** What kind of change this is: bug fix, new feature, breaking change, etc.

Pull requests should have all of this information laid out for lead developers to follow up on and for code reviewers to understand the motivation behind the change. Check out the relevant chapters for more information on pull request info and doing successful code reviews.

The only thing to watch out for is where your pull request needs to be merged into. Remember, features and bugs get merged back into the `develop` branch, and hotfixes get merged into `master`. Other than that, there is nothing special.

Merging and Deleting

Once a pull request is approved, merge it and close out the corresponding issue. Enjoy! Your issue is now sitting in the `develop` branch and will eventually be released to customers.

What if you did a hotfix? That hotfix got merged into `master`, but that bug still exists in `develop`. What do we do? Simple—we merge it into `develop` as well.

GitHub does not have a way to facilitate this, so this means either making a second pull request to `develop`, or just manually merging it in. I normally opt to manually merge it back up into `develop` to avoid having to do another approval process. It is a bit of a cheat, but the pull request was already approved once.

Releasing

Eventually, the code building up in `develop`—or that was just merged into `master`—needs to go out. The process is much like you would expect—just merge `develop` down into `master`, and create a new tag with the new version number. Your hotfix just gets tagged since it was already merged into `master`. You can then release the code out into the world!

Some people like to create a release branch before merging down into `master`. The idea is that this branch can be fully locked down so new features cannot go into it, and only bugfixes for things in the release can be applied. This branch can be useful in cases where you can schedule a sort of "feature freeze" in a project to iron out problems.

An Enjoyable Workflow

I have used this general workflow for many years, and have been quite happy with it. It is flexible enough to work on various types of projects, be they software-as-a-service (SaaS), applications, client work, or libraries. They are open enough that developers can focus on getting their tasks done without worrying too much about the process, but what little process exists can help immensely when looking at branches or getting 10,000-foot views.

This workflow can be augmented to work with just about any team, and you should give it a try. I hope it works as well for you as it does me.

Chapter

Reviewing Code

Code reviews are one of the best ways to help a team ensure they're writing the best code possible. In all of the jobs where we have done peer-lead code reviews, we have caught more bugs and had better discussions about code than in places or times where we just hammer code through the approval process. I know, I know; we all write beautiful, bug-free code, so why go through the hassle of a code review?

Think of code reviews as analogous to test-driven development. In TDD, we write tests so we can confidently say we didn't break anything, and provide an additional layer of documentation for how we expect code to work. The computer ends up being our second set of eyes continually watching for regressions in our application. If you use TDD, you know how nice it is to refactor some code, run tests, and know whether or not your refactoring worked or even made sense.

TDD also has a side effect of making you think about the architecture of your code. You will spend more time designing and laying out classes and structure than blindly coding until it works. This planning leads to more maintainable and cleaner code.

Code reviews provide a second set of eyes looking at the architecture and intent of code you write. If I am working on an issue, I may make some assumptions about how the system works, what users may or may not want to put up with, or just get too familiar with the code to notice things that need

9. Reviewing Code

to be changed. Having another person look at the code can expose logic bugs or structural issues a computer just cannot see.

Performing code reviews can give you a better view of parts of code you do not generally work on. I review Python code from many of my coworkers quite a bit, and it helps me understand some of the changes they are making on their side of the application. I can better anticipate when we need to make changes on the PHP side of the application based on the code they are working on, and we can have better discussions about the direction of the software.

Code reviews will slow down how quickly code makes it into the mainline portion of your software, but I find the benefits—maintainable code understood by more than one person—far outweigh the downsides.

Code Review Tools

Most source code hosting systems provide a mechanism for code reviews. I think the built-in tools for GitHub and Gitlab work reasonably well, and I more than likely already have other tools wired into these systems helping me with code management, like Jenkin's Pipeline system to handling automated testing. These default code review tools are usually more than capable of doing what I need, but there are some other options out there as well.

While I outline how to work with GitHub and GitLab, I highly suggest using tools that integrate directly with your workflow. For example, if you are using the Atlassian ecosystem, look at their Crucible code review tool. Any tool that integrates deeply into your existing software stack should provide you with a better overall experience than trying to bolt on random tools.

GitHub/GitHub Enterprise

Setup

Setting up a branch for code reviews is relatively simple, if somewhat hidden. By default, any PR can have comments on it and only collaborators can merge a PR. But you can go a step further and enforce that reviews are done. Doing so gives you the added benefit of being able to control when something is going to get merged and make sure someone has looked at it and given it a once over.

To enable reviews, go into the **Settings** for your project. On the left-hand menu, click on **Branches**. Here you'll find a section called *Protected Branches*. Now, we can turn on the code review enforcement.

Choose a branch from the drop-down, and Github forwards you to a configuration screen (see Figure 1). The first thing you want to do is check the **Protect This Branch** option. This opens up the rest of the configuration settings. You can now check **Require pull request views before merging**. This is the minimal amount you have to do, so you can click **Save Changes** at the bottom. Now any PRs made against the selected branch will have to have a code review applied.

Code Review Tools

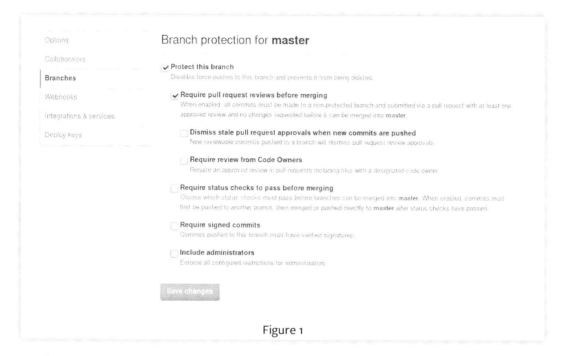

Figure 1

If you want, you can also enforce other rules. I generally also turn on **Dismiss stale pull request approvals when new commits are pushed**. This makes it so if I approve a PR, but then someone pushes more code to that branch before I merge it, it revokes the approval. This precaution is a good idea—and I think it should be on by default. You do not want someone to approve a PR then slide some additional code in at the last minute.

I do not particularly like the **Require review from Code Owner** option as I do not think it completely necessary for someone to be a gatekeeper for a feature or a set of code. That leads to siloing of information and tribal knowledge, which might not get passed on. If someone wants to review a block of code they are not hugely familiar with, they can ask for help or converse with the "code owner" about particulars. I much prefer everyone being able to look at, modify, and critique any part of a codebase.

Reviewing PRs

Once you've configured the reviews, we need a PR that is trying to merge into your newly protected branch. When creating a new PR, you can assign a reviewer then, or you can assign a reviewer later on.

When someone generates a new PR against a protected branch, just above the comment box on the "Conversation" tab will be a big red X and messages stating that a review is required and that the PR cannot be merged until it has at least one approved review.

9. Reviewing Code

Anyone can perform a review on a PR by going to the "Files Changed" tab of the PR and clicking "Review Changes." You can provide overall feedback and approve or reject the PR. You can also go down and commit on specific lines of code to start a review. At the end of your review, you will need to either approve or reject the PR.

If you have general comments, you can leave them without needing to do a formal review. I do not do actual reviews until I am entirely ready to either reject or approve a PR, since GitHub gets a bit funky about dismissing rejected reviews with no code commits. A good example is just asking a question about a line of code for clarification but then rejecting the PR overall. GitHub does not like to allow you to dismiss that rejection since no code was changed.

GitLab

Setup

I could not find any formal setup for enforcing code reviews in GitLab. The discussion tools are available right from the time a PR is generated, much like the general GitHub comment tools. The big difference is there is no way to prevent merging a PR until completing a code review. This is not the end of the world. However, it may require you to do more policing to make sure PRs are not going in before they have been reviewed.

> Merge request approvals[1] are available in the Enterprise edition of GitLab but not the Community Edition.

Reviewing PRs

Since the community edition of GitLab is more freeform than GitHub, there is more of an onus on the developers to follow a workflow than having the tools handle workflow for you.

The first step is to submit a PR and assign it to someone to review. This reviewer will go through the code and comment on individual lines. In GitLab, this will generate *Discussions*, and you should resolve all of these discussions by the time the PR is ready to be merged. The first task will be for the primary reviewer to go through the code, comment on any lines or changes needing clarification, and then pass it back to the original developer for changes, explanation, or debate.

When the original owner gets the PR back, they can respond to any of the discussions that have been started. This response can be in the form of code changes or further conversation. Each discussion has a **Resolve Discussion** button that can close it out.

Once you've resolved all of the discussions, you can merge the PR.

Keep in mind a PR can be merged at any time, as active and open discussions will not stop merging a PR.

---

[1] Merge request approvals: http://phpa.me/gitlab-merge-approval

Code Review in Practice

This is technology, so there are some practices you can follow to make sure that code review goes as smoothly, no matter which side of the review process you're on.

Don't Punish

First and foremost, code reviews are not the time to punish or call out developers. The entire point of a code review is to help each other write the best code possible, and demeaning comments or attacks in a code review are a no-go. It makes people not want to go through the review process for fear of being singled out. You should also watch your tone during the code review. Because you don't have body language and tone, text makes it easier to misinterpret comments as attacks; try and be helpful and make sure comments do not seem accusatory.

Ask Questions

You should ask questions about anything of which you are unsure. Things that are clear to me as the original developer might not be apparent to the reviewer; questions are a good thing. They can show potential clarity issues with the code, which can lead to maintenance problems down the line. In the worst-case scenario, a question might lead to a code change, but it might also lead to a simple response and explanation.

Have Clear Intentions

In either questions or recommendations, be clear about your intentions. Vague comments can just muddy the waters, especially if changes need to be made. Make it clear what the issue is and how you think it can be resolved. In the same vein, the original author might have a different way of fixing the problem. Compromise is a big deal, and we are all adults. Getting code accepted is not a win/lose situation. Work on a common fix.

No One "Owns" Code

Avoid the concept of "code ownership." I mention it a bit above, but when someone takes ownership of code, it leads to rougher peer reviews. By considering code "mine," you will be much more guarded against suggestions and changes than you might be about someone else's code. Even if another developer built a large chunk of the code you're working on, everyone is working on the same project. Feel free to consult or even have the original author perform the review, but neither side should assume just because someone wrote the code initially that it is in some way "holy" or "perfect."

Provide a Full Review

When you are reviewing code, make sure you are providing a review of all of the code that you can, not just a single class or file. If you are not, just leave comments or questions. Nothing is more frustrating than resolving a bunch of comments only to have more appear just because the original reviewer did not look at all of the code. Each review should be a full review of all of the code.

9. Reviewing Code

Remember to not only look at the syntax of the code, but also its architecture. Provide feedback on different tools or ways of performing the same actions. Is a class doing too much? Suggest breaking it into smaller classes, or suggest alternative libraries to use.

GitLab has a great article on performing code reviews[2]. I highly suggest reading through it in addition to my tips here.

Now Start Reviewing Code

I hope all of this helps convince you code reviews are a good idea, and that you can begin implementing them in either your open source contributions or at your place of work. Code reviews can be as simple as looking over code before it goes out, without any specialized set of tools. If you have dedicated tools, it can be more controlled and be another gatekeeper to making sure the best possible code is going out.

---

[2] *performing code reviews:* http://phpa.me/gitlab-code-review

Chapter 10

Finding Someone New

There will come a time when you will need to add to your team. It can be due to a team member leaving, the workload growing to more than your team can handle, or just because you want to expand what your team does. In any of those cases, you will need to start the arduous task of finding someone new to bring to your team.

This process can be time-consuming, but in the end, it should be worth it to bring on a new team member. I have done hiring in the past, so here are my thoughts and tips for helping find that new team member.

Describing the Job

I hate writing job descriptions; most of the time, they are long-winded and vague. We want to hire a coder. It should be that easy, right?

I wish it were. Writing a good job description takes skill and practice, and there are a few things to keep in mind when writing a job description. You will need to put on your best salesperson hat along with your developer hat to come up with something engaging, but that reflects what the job is about.

Most importantly, be honest. This is a sticking point for me. In the job description, describe exactly what the potential hire will be doing. I do not like to hide job responsibility behind vague

10. Finding Someone New

phrases like "fast-paced, challenging environment" or "perform other tasks as needed." Once you start looking for mid or senior level people, they see right through most of the glittery language.

Avoid language like "rock star" or "ninja," most developers look right past these terms and could dismiss your job entirely. Unless you want me to get wasted and trash hotel rooms, you are not looking for a developer. You are looking for a developer with experience. You are not looking for a developer no one notices and delivers code in the middle of the night, you probably want a team player.

Do list out what the job title will be. Unless it's actually going to be "Rockstar Developer," do not put that down. If you are hiring for a Senior Developer, put that down. Your HR department might have a say in how it's worded but use the actual title. A brief description will also be helpful as it can help differentiate a junior from a mid-level developer.

Write down the key responsibilities. Are developers expected to do code reviews? Write that down. Should they be able to write technical documentation? That goes in too. If the job requires travel to clients, include it. If the new hire is expected to be evaluated on it from a performance perspective, write it down.

When it comes to skills and qualifications, be specific in what you want. When I hired someone new last year, I included that I needed a developer with PHP experience but some JavaScript knowledge. While we also do Python work on a different part of a codebase, it was not required for the job. Be realistic in what you are looking for as well. A junior developer will not have five years of experience in a single language, let alone multiple languages. Keep in mind these qualifications are the best possible things you want; you should not use them as an absolute gate against potential hires.

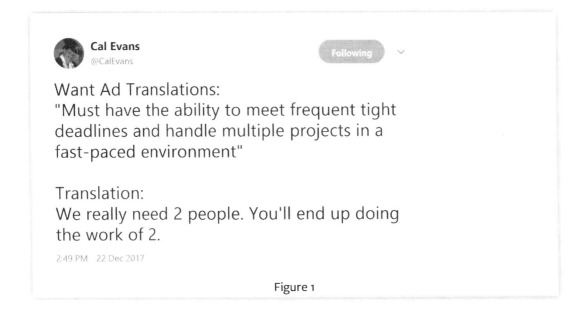

Figure 1

Specify if this is a remote position or not. As someone who only works remotely, I hate applying for a job only to find out remote is not a possibility. As more and more people want to have a small commute, or not move at all, listing the location of the job and its availability for remote work is critical.

Finally, list whether or not the position is a direct hire, and whether it is part-time or full time. When I was last looking for a new job, I had to decline many second interviews as I found out after the fact the positions were contract-only. Don't waste your own or a potential hire's time when the expectation for the type of employment is vague.

Building a Network

The best way to find a new candidate is to build up a network of people around you. I would not be in the position I am in right now if I didn't meet new people when I went to conferences or training. Even if it only means following them on Twitter or LinkedIn, building up a network is a massive boon to finding a new hire. When you have an open position, they might be interested themselves or might help find people interested via their contacts. In the tech industry, it is not uncommon for a good chunk of people to always be on the lookout for new opportunities. When I have tweeted out about a job, I get a decent combination of retweets as well as direct inquiries.

Doing so is a helpful way to start gathering prospective hires. I am more likely to take a personal recommendation for an interview than strictly off of a resume. I will get to resumes in just a moment, but someone vouching for someone else is priceless. If someone says, "This might be a good fit, you should talk!" I will more than likely spend additional time vetting that potential hire than I would with just a sent in resume.

Having an extensive network also means you have a better chance of finding someone at the skill level you are looking for. While most of my friends are senior-level developers, I am more than likely hiring for junior or mid-level developers. They might be able to recommend someone, or even with a retweet bring in someone from their network.

Building out your network will take a bit of social grace. First, meet and talk to people at conferences, training, local user groups, or other places where you meet fellow developers. From there, follow them on Twitter or your social network of choice. I mainly use Twitter and reserve LinkedIn mostly for actual work relationships or people I have worked directly with or known for a long time; Facebook is strictly a "friend" place. LinkedIn is generally a good place to follow people as it can also help lead to new links through a common social network.

Do not hound your network when you are looking for new hires. Write posts and tweets explaining you're looking, but I find that unless I'm specifically looking for someone—whom I will contact directly—I let the natural virality of shares and retweets do their thing. This has been reasonably successful in the past.

10. Finding Someone New

Working With Recruiters

It may be beneficial to work with a recruiter. I admit I am biased, but having tried to use recruiters to find a job, I'm always wary of using recruiters to help find a potential hire. Not only have I been burned by a recruiter sending me on a completely useless interview, but many recruiters think the best way to find someone is just to recommend everyone.

Finding a good recruiter can be hard, but it is possible. Like building your network, talk to the recruiter. Find out what circles they travel in, and what sort of technical areas they specialize in. A good recruiter does not need to know how to code, but they should understand what programming is and what makes a good programmer. A good recruiter will work with you to find a candidate, not just shove resumes in your face.

Recruiters may show up at local conferences or user groups. Take the time to talk to them and find out more about what they do. Trust your instincts; if something smells fishy, don't use them. If you can find a good, competent recruiter, they can be invaluable for helping weed out bad fits.

Going Through Resumes

Going through resumes is a tough task. Hopefully, you end up with a stack of them to go through, and hopefully, that stack is not too high. I remember years ago looking to hire a new developer; the pile of resumes was nearly six inches thick. Out of that stack, we only found about ten good resumes, and only a few made it through to a second interview. It can be a slog.

First, you need to weed out poorly written ones. If your resume contains spelling and grammar mistakes, it is an automatic pass. A resume is the first impression of a person. If the first impression shows they are not taking the time to proof-read what should get them an initial interview, how well will they be at the actual job? A developer has to have strong written communication skills, even if they are not doing much technical work. Much of the time, developers communicate through textual mediums; a poorly written resume generally means their day-to-day communications will not be much better.

From there, you will need to match a person's qualifications to the position you want to fill. This requires a personal touch, and you can be as strict or generous with how much a candidate should match. If you are hiring for a junior developer role for a PHP position, but the person only knows C#, that should not automatically disqualify them. "Junior developer" should be a learning position anyway. If you are hiring for a senior position requiring PHP, JavaScript, and Ruby, someone who knows C#, Python, and PHP might still be a decent fit as senior developers can adapt to new languages without too much effort.

I am not someone who prescribes to letting a flashy resume through. During my last round of hiring where we were looking for a new Python developer, I had plenty of nice, fancy looking resumes. The only ones that got selected were the ones with the appropriate experience. A nicely formatted, clear, and easy-to-read resume will always win with me more than a colorful, whimsical one.

The First Interview

The first interview should be a combination of getting to know someone and a baseline technical overview of what they know. Take the time to verify the candidate's resume matches their experience. I have heard plenty of stories where a recruiter has massaged a resume to fit a position unbeknownst to the interviewee. I have seen people overstate their experience on their resume, so this is a good time to validate the resume.

Go over the job description with them to make sure they understand the position itself. Walk them through a typical day and see if it matches up with their expectations. A nicely written, clear job posting can still be interpreted differently by different people. You may have an idea of what a mid-level developer is, and that may not be what the interviewee was expecting.

Take the time to find out the requirements and expectations of the person you interview. For example, I always let potential employers know I frequently present at conferences and would like to continue doing so. Some companies are okay with their employees traveling to speak; some are not. If you offer a remote position, find out what the potential hire thinks that entails, or what they might need to be able to do their job. How does travel work for them? Are they okay with a potentially long commute?

Find out the type of work the person has done historically. Go through their resume, asking about finer points with their experience. Now is the time to find out that while the person worked on a big project, maybe their role was not as impactful as the resume made it sound. Listen to what the interviewee is excited to discuss, and which things they shun away from expanding upon.

Be honest about the job, but remember you are still in the sales phase of finding a new hire. Talk up the company, why you like working there, and the advantages of the company. Talk about the types of projects you and the new hire will be working on. Make the interviewee as excited to work at your company as you are.

Lay all the facts about the job on the table, including potential pay ranges. Don't waste anyone's time. If a position is great and the person is a good fit, but I am not paying enough, both myself and the interviewee should be able to cut the process short. It is no use to do a phone interview, followed by an in-person interview, to then find out you are paying way less than the person wants. Also, explain benefits so applicants can get a feel for the entire compensation package.

Keep accurate notes during this interview. Once you have done all the first rounds of interviews, take a step back and go through all the notes. Which hires sounded like they had potential? Which ones did not fit? You will need to decide which ones move on to the next phase.

The Second Interview

The second interview can take many forms, but this is generally a more in-depth technical interview and is almost always in person. Have the potential hire come out to the company and meet them face-to-face. Remember, this is stressful for the interviewee, so keeping to a schedule and making sure everything goes smoothly should be a top priority.

10. Finding Someone New

During the technical interview, you will be gauging not only technical prowess but also company fit. Have the person meet with the team they will be working on so they can converse and see how well they get along. If you hire this person, they will be working with the team. Now is the best time to start seeing how it all works together.

I like to do a combination of technical and social interviewing. I am not huge on writing out code on a whiteboard, and I never ask someone to write out how to implement a sorting algorithm without any help. Even I cannot remember how to do them half the time. What I do ask is for the candidate to describe, in depth, something they worked on that was important to them. Draw out how it worked. Explain the complexities of the problem and how they were solved. *Why* was this a project they enjoyed working on?

Have them do the same thing for a project they hated. Asking this is an excellent way to get someone to explain technical details on why something did not work, or why something was more complicated than it was initially thought to be. An honest answer could be that it was a management issue, but if they can explain it articulately, that's always a plus. If they go on a tirade about how management sucked and it was all their fault, that might be a red flag.

I find these two questions to be a great way to figure out the thought process of an interviewee, and a much better way than asking the typical questions like, "How would you move Mt. Fuji?"

Depending on your team's size, do multiple interviews with small chunks of the team or with the entire team. Have them meet with you, team members, maybe even your boss or someone higher ranking than yourself.

Each company is a bit different when it comes to their second interviews, but overall this is the time to get deep with the interviewee. The goal of the second interview is to see how well the person interacts with the team, what their actual technical level is, and how well they figure out problems.

The Offer

At this point, you have hopefully found the hire you want. You and the potential hire have already talked about pay ranges, what the benefits of the company are, and the responsibilities. Now is the time to write all of that up as a formal offer. Get whomever you need to sign off on it, and send it off.

Negotiations are a fact of life when it comes to hiring. Do not be stymied when someone comes back with a counteroffer. Work with your company to either negotiate further or move on. I have a set range I can move around in when I do hires, and I am interested in paying what the person is worth, not just what the company wants. This reason is why I explain this all in the first interview. If I'm paying a mid-developer salary but want a senior developer, it frequently leads to negotiation friction.

Hopefully, the candidate you wanted most accepts the offer. If not, do not take it personally. Someone's expectations change, or the interviewee had a change of heart about the position. Move on to the next person on the list.

If all goes as planned, you should have a new hire!

Onboarding

Next, let's discuss onboarding new hires and what your team can do to help. Good onboarding practices benefit the entire team, whether there's a new hire on the horizon or not.

Chapter 11

Coming Aboard!

The need to onboard new hires is one of the most significant reasons why adding workers to a project does not increase the project's productivity. It takes time to get them up to speed with how the system works, what their role is, day-to-day workflows, and a host of other things. The goal of any new hire, even ones where you aren't trying to fill in gaps during emergencies, is to get new hires as productive as possible as quickly as possible.

Onboarding is the process a new hire goes through as soon as they are hired. The more smoothly this process goes, the quicker the hire becomes a fully productive member of the team. It has its bounds on efficiency, but whenever a new hire comes in, we should be doing our utmost as developer leads to make sure they are taken care of and given the attention and information they need.

> *"Adding manpower to a late software project makes it later."*
> – Brooks's Law, Fred Brooks

11. Coming Aboard!

Be Organized

Nothing is worse than coming in on the first day and sitting around, having no idea what to do. I know, because it has happened to me.

If your company has a document store like Google Drive, Dropbox, or Microsoft Office OneDrive, collect and store all the onboarding documentation in one place. When the new employee shows up on day one, they can have access to this document store and have everything at their fingertips. An employee should be able to comb through this with some direction and hit the ground running on the first day.

> *Of course, we're talking about onboarding a new team member to how your team works. You'll also have to coordinate with someone else in the company to get benefits, tax forms, identification, and other related human resources tasks taken care of. Make sure this part is organized as well since a new employee will be anxious about taking care of these too.*

At my current employer, we have a document called "Springboard" which is our primary onboarding document, inside a folder containing various other useful materials. This document links to multiple folders in our Google Drive, the first steps you need to take, and information helpful in getting set up. The documentation also contains information on setting up a VPN connection.

Along these lines, this is where documentation of the projects really should come to the forefront. The onboarding documentation should give clear links to the application help and technical documentation so a new employee can quickly find information about the work they will be doing. A new employee should be able to ask for help and will need some direction, but the more documentation and support they have access to, the quicker they can figure out what is going on. It goes without saying. You should keep this documentation up to date. When you have a new team member joining, make time to review your onboarding documentation.

You should have a plan for the first thirty days for a new employee. If you have clear objectives, both you and the new employee know what you expect of them and what work they will be doing. This step does not need to be a task with a hard deadline. Knowing that the first week is planned to be setup time, the second week is bug triaging and the first pull requests, the third week is coming up with OKRs and other long-term objectives, and week four would be the first set of overall reviews all help you and the new employee make sure they are on track.

The Hardware and Software

One of the most significant pain points for developers is not having the proper hardware and software they need to do their jobs effectively. Prior to a new developer coming on board, you should find out what kind of hardware and software they expect. At my employer, there are no mandatory pieces of software you have to run beyond our VPN software, which is open source and runs on everything. Other than that, we have no hard restrictions.

After hiring an employee, find out what kind of hardware they expect, and temper that with whatever restrictions your company has, and make sure everything is all set up for the new employee on day one. Unless there is a good reason to deviate, try to accommodate the employee as much as possible. Most shops I have worked at were more interested in me having a productive setup than whether or not I am running Windows on specific, cheap hardware. On just my team alone, we have: me, with a desktop and a laptop running Linux; one of my coworkers working from a Microsoft Surfacebook; and second on a Windows machine. Our designer switches between Windows and a Mac.

We try to use as many cross-platform tools as possible to help minimize OS and software lock-in. Now that Windows 10 supports a full Linux command line, it is less of a hassle, but there are also tools like Vagrant and Docker which help standardize tooling across platforms. I make sure our development environments work on as many platforms as possible.

For PHP development, you can use just about any combination of hardware and operating system. Still, if you are in a more corporate environment that, for example, uses Active Directory—a brand new MacBook might be hard to manage. I have worked in places where there were restrictions on branding, such as using Dell for all the hardware, or preferences for Apple over typical PC hardware, and that's fine. Those are things to consider, but remember, developers have different needs than normal users—high amounts of RAM, fast I/O, good screens, ideally admin or root access, and higher-end hardware. If you can meet these needs, your developers will be much more productive.

Don't skimp on hardware. The one downside to allowing an employee to pick the hardware they want is they might choose something not that great. At an agency I worked for, one developer used an older HP laptop with almost no RAM and a CPU that did not allow hardware virtualization. He selected it at the time because it was cheap, and he didn't want to have the company spend a bunch of money on hardware for him to run a text editor. When we switched to a Vagrant setup, we struggled quite a bit to bring him up to speed.

If an employee does not have any specific recommendations, find out the operating system and whether they would like a desktop or a laptop. From there, you can get good quality, higher-end hardware for them. For Apple users, get a good MacBook Pro or iMac (especially since they are not upgradeable in a meaningful way). For Linux users, Thinkpads, System 76, or Dell tend to work well, and for Windows users, the Microsoft Surfacebook, Dell XPS, and Razer lines offer excellent hardware with good battery life.

Assign a Buddy

On teams that are large enough, assign a buddy to the new employee. This buddy will be the bridge point for the new employee to meet their coworkers but also act as a guiding point for what to do in the first crucial weeks. This buddy will not only provide some guidance on getting set up and the general workflow of the day-to-day operations but also work as a sounding board and someone they can easily approach for technical questions. The buddy should be someone on the team, but not a boss, supervisor, or the CTO. Make sure it's someone the new person can go to for advice and won't feel shy or hesitant about asking basic questions.

11. Coming Aboard!

Having someone to help mentor a new employee can be a big difference between someone struggling to wrap their head around all this new code and someone who will start to feel confident in what they are doing. While the buddy may sacrifice their workday to help out the new employee, the traction the new employee gains will be more than made up in the lost productivity of the mentor. I would much rather have a mentor spending time with a brand-new employee knowing the short-term impact is worth getting them productive quicker.

The buddy can also help the new employee from a social aspect. The buddy will check in with the new employee and see how they are doing, if they have any questions, and can help direct them to other people in the company. The new employee can also ask who different people are, with the buddy providing a stepping stone to meeting the other employees. This is especially crucial in remote situations where someone has to start working with people and never sees their faces. At one job, I went about two months before meeting most of the team outside of my own.

Buffer, a product that helps with managing scheduled social media posts, uses a three buddy system[1] where they pair up a new employee with a Leader Buddy, a Role Buddy, and a Culture Buddy. The Leader Buddy is mostly in charge of the onboarding of the new employee, validating the hire was a good fit for the company and is sort of a mentor to the other buddies. The Role Buddy helps the new employee with and understand their role in the company. The Culture Buddy helps the new employee "fit in" with the rest of the company by providing more social and company information to the new employee.

The size of your team will impact whether you go with a one or many buddy type of system, but having someone around to show the new employee the ropes is always a great addition.

Getting Going

The best way for a new employee to begin to understand a new system is to have them start working on something meaningful that is work they would be doing for the role. Instead of having them work on meaningless fluff, or spend time just reading, give the new employee tickets to work on. These do not need to be gigantic projects but start with bug and maintenance fixes. These give the new employee a chance to poke around in the system and ask questions.

I do generally reserve the first few days for a new employee to get everything set up, including hardware and software, but then they should be able to start working. These issues should be something that either exposes the new employee to various parts of the system or requires something much more meaningful than simple typo fixing. These issues will make sure the new employee has everything set up, their tooling is correctly wired, and that they can effectively debug the application.

When a new employee is hired, go through existing issues and start tagging ones that would be suitable first issues. I particularly like bugs because they force the new employee to figure out how to debug the new application. While PHP does have excellent tools like Xdebug for debugging, you need

---

[1] three buddy system: _https://open.buffer.com/?p=2347_

to get your environment set up so it runs, and you have a way to interact with it. After debugging a bug, the new employee can write tests and then actually fix the bug.

A mentor/buddy really comes in handy for a new hire here. The buddy can help the new hire with where to look for the bugs, issues on getting set up, pointing in the right directions for documentation, and all those things the new hire will need for updating the code and accompanying documentation. The unit tests provide a quick way to validate the bug has been appropriately fixed but also gives the new hire a good idea of how the rest of the system works.

Which leads us to code reviews.

Code Reviews

Code reviews are not just an onboarding task, but they do provide a quick feedback loop to the new hire. Read Chapter 9 for a more in-depth discussion on _code reviews_, but in general, a code review will give the new employee a chance to ask questions and find out how well their code is written. A code review is always a chance for someone to improve their work but should never be a way to punish or put down any employee. Code reviews are a great time to start building good habits for the new employee and introduce them to workflows.

A useful code review will go over the original issue and make sure it was correctly fixed. The new employee can be made aware of potential bugs or problems with their code and be notified of potential impacts on the rest of the system. A good example may be a system which generates reports, and while the fix may be correct, it may be inefficient in a production setting.

The code review can also help fill in knowledge gaps for the new hire. There may be an existing library or some other code that might be helpful. From a developer lead point-of-view, it also gives an insight into how the new hire works and how well they fit into their role.

Most companies are now using tools like GitHub, Bitbucket, or GitLab that provide excellent tools for doing code reviews. With the proliferation of hosted source code repositories like Github and Gitlab, there does seem to be a dearth of offline or non-hosted code review products. If there are ones you use, I would love to know. However, the tools built into GitHub or whatever code repository host you use should suffice. GitHub especially tends to push the envelope on these tools, and the others soon follow.

Better Productivity Through Better Onboarding

These onboarding tips will help you as your team grows and you bring on more people as efficiently as possible. There is no quick way to bring someone to one-hundred-percent efficiency, but there are plenty of things we can do to make a new hire have a smooth experience. With a bit of planning, some documentation, and a sound support system, a new hire should feel comfortable in their new role in your company.

Chapter 12

Measuring Success

There will come a time, probably once a year per team member, when you will have to assess how well a team member is working. Are they contributing overall to the team? Are they making their goals? Do they know what their goals are? Are they pulling their weight?

As long as companies have existed, there has been a need to quantify how well an individual employee performs. "Gut feeling" is not the most accurate way to do this. There are also many ways which do not work in real-world situations.

So what options do we have?

Useless Metrics

First and foremost, go ahead and throw out any measurement solely dependant on things like how many lines of code a person has added to the codebase, how many "story points" or issues a person resolves or sprint, or any arbitrary number by itself.

Metrics like the above can easily be gamed. As such, they do not prove anything when looked at on their own. If Bob completes ten issues, and Tom completes three, did Bob do more work than

12. Measuring Success

Tom? If Alice added four thousand lines of code, but Jan only added fifteen hundred, did Alice do more work than Jan?

What these metrics do not tell you is any sort of context on how the work was completed. It does not tell you Bob completed ten issues, but six of those were simple text changes, three of them were "Closed, Won't Fix" because they were old versions of the software, and the final issue was a basic feature which took him a day to work on.

Tom spent two weeks on three major issues for customers, each of which will help bring in increased customer satisfaction. With this additional context, it is clear that Tom potentially did more work than Bob, even though he worked on fewer issues.

As I mentioned, metrics can easily be gamed. Have you ever had a support call just disconnect in the middle? Many call centers have goals for the length of time a call should last, and if a support tech is over the average, then they get penalized.

Since there is little you can do to them, if the support tech reaches the maximum time limit, they just put you on hold and disconnect the call. The tech's numbers will not reflect 80% of their support calls were unresolved, only that they achieved their average time.

Bottom line—ignore tracking progress and success with basic metrics.

SMART

Management By Objectives, or MBO, is a process of defining goals and objectives, created by Peter Drucker in the book *The Practice of Management*[1]. It has been mostly superseded by a newer style called OKR, which I will talk about in the next section. One thing born out of the MBO process was the idea of using SMART to determine goals. SMART stands for:

- **S**pecific
- **M**easurable
- **A**chievable
- **R**elevant
- **T**ime bound

Using the above criteria, each goal given to a team member should be relevant to their current tasks and the goals of management. The goals should not be superfluous or abstract but concrete goals that can be tracked, measured, and evaluated at the end of a period.

Goals should be specific and not abstract. You should be able to articulate what you want to accomplish, why it is important, and what limits or who it affects. The goal should have some metric to measure by so you know when the goal is accomplished. The goal should be achievable, even if the achievement is a bit of a stretch. The goal should be relevant to what you are doing, not just a thing for a person to do. Finally, a goal should have a deadline like the end of a quarter, or ninety days, or end of the year.

---

[1] *The Practice of Management:* https://amazon.com/dp/B003F1WM8E

At the end of the agreed-upon time limit, you should be able to measure the individual goal and see if it was reached. If it was not, you can deal with it. If it was, you can reward the team member.

Work with each team member to come up with a relevant set of goals. In today's work environment, a quick turn around is valuable, so set goals on a quarterly or monthly basis. Make sure the goals themselves are achievable within the time frame, as goals should *not* be used as a form of punishment or a way to force someone to fail.

OKRs

OKRS, or *Objectives and Key Results*[2], are a fairly common way for an organization to keep track of goals at various levels. OKRs generally flow downhill, so an individual may have company OKRs, team OKRs, and even possibly personal OKRs they need to be aware of.

A good template for OKRs is one objective and three measurable results. These quantifiable results are set per quarter and should help a person move toward the overall goal. I am a fan of the objective being a management set ideal, where the results are worked out at a much more individual level.

One sort of unique thing about OKRs is they are not generally something one hundred percent achievable. Fully completing two of the measurable results is the general goal, and if all three results are achieved, then it should signify a considerable achievement.

Key results are not just a list of things to do—they should be something requiring real work and should help move a person toward their overall objective. These should also be concrete and measurable.

For example, a team may set an overall goal of increasing code confidence. Bob and Alice sit down to work out Bob's goals for the quarter, and they decide on three things for Bob to work on. The objective is abstract, but the key results should be something Bob and Alice can track.

First, Bob should set a goal of sixty percent of his pull requests including unit tests. The percentage is based on the fact the codebase is relatively old and not easily tested, so there is some forgiveness when working on maintenance tasks.

Second, Bob should have ninety percent of his pull requests code reviewed. This is not a punishment for bad code, but for Bob to make sure he works with the rest of the team, and his code is visible and being reviewed. Having the team more knowledgeable about his work will help them better understand the overall codebase.

Finally, all of Bob's pull requests should include documentation updates. Again, the idea is not seen as a punishment but as an overall goal to help increase the visibility of code, how the software works, and helps ensure everyone has the most up-to-date knowledge of how the application works.

The rest of the team will have similar key results, or at least key results helping them move toward an overall goal of better code confidence. Even getting only two out of the three results completed still helps move everyone toward the agreed-upon objective.

---

[2]   *Objectives and Key Results*: http://www.eisenhower.me/okr/

12. Measuring Success

One book commonly recommended is Radical Focus: Achieving Your Most Important Goals with Objectives and Key Results[3]. I recommend reading this book if you are interested in setting up OKRs for your team or organization.

360-Degree Peer Reviews

Peer reviews are nothing new, but at least in the companies I have been a part of, peer reviews were generally used as an anonymous comment system to complain about team members. When done properly, peer reviews can be an effective way to gauge team member interaction and get information not readily visible from a management perspective.

Years ago, I worked for an ISP, and every year I was there, I generally received overall positive comments, except from one person. This person complained about my lack of procedural knowledge and my inability to deal with customers on my own. This person was the billing manager and hated when I sent angry customers with billing issues to her. However, I was part of support, not billing.

Of course, *I* never saw a name on the peer review. Still, when the only other manager I dealt with was the billing manager, and my manager never complained about my ability to deal with customers, it was not hard to figure out. She was management, though, so to the owners and other managers, her comments pulled more weight than my coworkers.

Netflix has instituted the idea of 360-degree peer reviews[4], which collect feedback from team members, management, and subordinates in a signed format. This feedback is collected and then used as part of their review process. The big difference between what I experienced and what Netflix does is the lack of anonymity.

Netflix asks colleagues to list: something the reviewee should continue doing, something they should start, and something they should stop. Netflix uses this information in place of a formal review. Their thinking is that if everyone is honest with everyone else, you will end up with better results.

I would not base a review totally on comments, but peer reviews can be used to provide context for the work a team member has been doing.

Discovering and Dealing With Poor Performance

Unfortunately, there will come a time when you will have to deal with a struggling team member. In the best case, a consistent schedule of reviews and talking with team members—including the struggling member—should help expose issues quickly and allow you to deal with them efficiently. Sometimes the issues are personal, sometimes the issues are medical, and sometimes the concerns are just technical. It is up to you to help determine where to help the team member.

---

[3]   Radical Focus: Achieving Your Most Important Goals with Objectives and Key Results: https://www.amazon.com/dp/B01BFKJA0Y

[4]   360-degree peer reviews: http://phpa.me/hbr-netflix-hr

This is a crucial thing to remember—poor performance is not usually something which *has* to be punished. Given the benefit of the doubt, most people want to do a good job and be a productive member of the team. Poor performance is generally the result of some other influence, and identifying this influence can help both of you come up with a plan.

The correct course of action also somewhat depends on what the underlying issue is. If your company is using OKRs as a measuring stick, work with the team member to possibly generate more realistic key results. You should tailor each set of results to the individual team member. However, someone who is not meeting their results has to have a reason. It could be the results are just out of their reach. Do they consistently miss technical-based results? Are they missing personal organization results?

In the above case, if Bob is consistently having issues with his technical goals, maybe make only one of his goals the technical one, and have it be his stretch goal. Perhaps Bob is just not getting how unit testing works, which is why he is not writing as many unit tests as he should. Additional training can help shore him up. There are plenty of books and tutorials out there to help teach test-driven development, so work with him to find one which works for him.

No matter what you do, I find it best to be honest. You do not have to be brutally honest when dealing with poor performance, but honesty really is the best policy. Do not lead someone to believe they are doing a good job when they are not. Doing so does not help them or the rest of the team. Be honest with where problems are, but also be willing to help fix the issues. Do not leave it up to the team member by themselves to come up with a solution.

Being honest also means the possibility the job or team is just not a good fit for a team member. This goal is one of the things Netflix strives for with its peer review system. If someone is not working out, let the person go on to find something better suited for them. While I have never worked there, I am sure the teams first try to improve performance before immediately hitting the "Fire" button.

I will quickly bring up the idea of *performance improvement plans* (PIPs). In short, they are concrete plans to help an employee improve an ongoing issue. If someone is consistently coming in late and talking with them about it is not working, a PIP may be put into place stating the employee needs to be on time for the next ninety days, barring medical or pre-approved reasons. Not being late for 90 days indicates successful completion of the PIP. Doing something like calling in and saying they have car trouble only to show up hours later and not making up time would be considered a failure.

In a more traditional setting outside of software development, I suppose they make sense. I do not like using PIPs for technical goals only because it helps enforce the meaningless metrics I said are useless on their own. Software development progression is tough to quantify into concrete numbers, and things like PIPs rely on numbers. I find something like an OKR works better than saying, "Bob must close at least ten issues a week" or "Bob must write at least 15 unit tests a week for ninety days." Both of those metrics can be gamed easily.

Still, PIPs used for more traditional issues like attendance, interaction with team members, and communication issues may be appropriate.

12. Measuring Success

There is no magic bullet for dealing with poor performance. As with everything else I have talked about in this column, communication is vital. Find out the core issues, try and resolve them, and go from there. Sometimes things improve, sometimes things do not.

What Works Best

As with many things I've discussed, take these ideas back to your team and start a dialogue. Modify them to work with your individual team and organization is something you will want buy-in from the top all the way to the bottom.

Even if none of these ideas jump out as the best for you and your team, remember, do not use anything you pick as a punishment. Stay away from being Dogbert and using measurements as a way to segment team members into "good" or "bad."

Use progress and success tracking as a way to make sure everyone is staying on the same page, and identify when someone is falling behind. An outcome may be a team member is indeed not a good fit, or cannot perform at the needed levels, and it's okay. Just do not use metrics as the end-all-be-all to make the determination.

Chapter 13

The Code Monkey

I once told a coworker that a [explitive] monkey could do a better job than he could.

I wasn't a team lead at the time, but I do not suggest you do that at any point during the work day, let alone during the middle of conflict resolution. There will come a time where you are going to have to deal with team members that are not satisfactory. It could be due to a variety of reasons, but constructively dealing with issues is an invaluable skill.

The Argument

How all this came about is nothing special. At the time, I was working with a coworker, who was primarily a network administrator who sometimes worked with the website. We—or more accurately, I—was working to move our business customer-facing website from a local ISP's hosted setup to a self-maintained, on-site server. We needed the flexibility of running whatever we wanted, which included code to talk to our back office system on an AS/400. We could not do that on a $5-month hosting plan.

13. The Code Monkey

As part of that move, we gained a few extra perks. One of those was a web server dedicated to running a PHP 5.1 application and had all the resources to itself. We could move away from the older one-PHP-file-per-page model to using a better-designed framework. This was before Symfony or Zend Framework had gained much traction. I had, of course, built my own framework.

It was a basic front controller system, and user-friendly, pretty URLs were not possible before the move. We could also utilize SSL, so our entire site could run under a wildcard SSL certificate. This point is where the argument began.

Back then, there was a somewhat valid argument about not running SSL on every page on your website and only running SSL on the pages needing encryption. SSL encryption does take CPU cycles and would reduce the amount of load our servers could handle. Now couple that with a bit fatter application by virtue of the front controller design. It was still in the days before PSR-0 and the widespread idea of autoloading, so we were using more memory.

We had our dedicated box with more than enough power, but technically we were using more resources. Usage monitors showed memory and CPU growth. None of the increase was near the limits of the box, but technically the number two is higher than the number one, even if your ceiling is one hundred. He took it upon himself to go to our CTO and complain. This being the first real complaint I had had about my performance or abilities, I took it in stride and explained the situation.

This coworker only worked sporadically on the website code. We did not have code reviews and did not have source control at the time. Files were just SCP'd (secure copied) to the production server when ready—one encrypted step up from plain FTP. I got a call from a board member saying something was not working on the site. I went to investigate.

What I found was a huge amount of copy-pasted code and a whole bunch of Dutch. My coworker had:

1. googled to find a tutorial,
2. copied and pasted the code, and
3. pushed to Production.

It's a software lifecycle I am sure we are all familiar with. A few other groups needed this feature, so each block of code was copy and pasted to where it needed to be procedurally, Dutch comments and all.

This process, for me, was the straw that broke the camel's back. I fixed the problem, documented it, and then went to the CTO. I had had enough. It was a combination of the copy-paste mentality, the blatant lack of trying, and the no testing that pushed me over to the edge. I complained.

My coworker was called into the office, and the charges leveled against him. His excuse was to say that he programs for efficiency and function calls cost CPU cycles. While he was on the subject, he returned to the CPU and memory usage increases we were seeing. He complained about the in-efficiency of our templating system, Smarty, and how we should be using static HTML files. If we keep letting me program this way, we were going to spend a fortune on hardware.

I will admit, I sat there with my jaw against the floor:

> *He does not believe in using functions because it costs CPU cycles?!*

We deployed to a dual-CPU server with 256 megabytes of RAM! (Yes, this was a while ago.) He had also not come from an era where performance and hardware were a premium. He had gone from Visual Basic 6 to PHP. So I uttered the words:

> *"A [explitive] monkey could code better than you."*

Dealing with Problems is Key

In this case, I think both myself and my coworker were in the wrong on various levels. My boss, the CTO, also failed, but in a vastly different way. On the one hand, my coworker was well out of his element. On the other hand, my insult was not the most professional way to go about bridging the subject. You will have to deal with coworkers that are not working well on the team, and that can be hard.

There is a good quote from *The New One Minute Manager*[1]:

> *"The managers who were interested in results often seemed to be labeled 'autocratic,' while the managers interested in people were often labeled 'democratic.' The young man thought each of these managers–the 'tough' autocrat and the 'nice' democrat–were only partially effective. 'It's like being half a manager,' he thought. He returned home tired and discouraged. He might have given up his search long ago, but he had one great advantage. He knew precisely what he was looking for. 'Effective managers,' he thought, 'manage themselves and the people they work with so that both the organization and the people profit from their presence.'"*

You need to be comfortable being autocratic. We all have goals that need to be accomplished, especially in a business setting. You cannot, and you should not, let poor performing developers just continue the way they are. Nothing will change, and you will never reach your goals. You need to confront these people.

At the same time, many leads think a hands-off approach is the best, as confrontation leads to ill feelings. If you have an unhappy team, they will perform less favorably, and your goals will not be met. Be friendly and accommodating, and everyone will be happy.

The real world does not work this way. The reason my entire situation happened was because there was no effective way to work on complaints until lodging formal ones. Part of this was the company culture—people that "rocked the boat" tended not to fare terribly well. It was easier just to keep your head down and put up with things that stunk. Problems grew until they finally explode, and one

---

[1] *The New One Minute Manager*: https://amazon.com/dp/0062367544

13. The Code Monkey

coworker tells another a monkey could do his job. Our managers, not just the CTO, took the "democratic" route and kept their hands clean of problems.

Being authoritarian and heavy-handed is not necessarily the answer either.

I came across a recent post titled *On being the employee who 'needs improvement*[2] by Avdi Grimm. In it, Avdi details that his bosses went directly to a strict Personal Improvement Plan after, in his own words, his bosses were "left hanging, waiting for a day or more on my work." Avdi mentions that he regularly took time off at will to handle family problems as he thought a remote position would allow. The tone seems to indicate that the core issue was that he would regularly disappear from work. He showed up to work when he wanted, not when he was expected.

His bosses, after half of a year, put him on a strict weekly performance review. They had not attempted to work with him or find out what Avdi's reasons for not being at work regularly were. It was an immediate punishment that soured Avdi's confidence in his employment and with the company.

The Middle of the Road

What I find is a middle of the road approach tends to do better. You need to be authoritarian enough to know when to put your foot down and make sure things are getting done on time, and problems are dealt with efficiently. You need to be democratic enough that issues can be talked about in an open space, and that problems are dealt with fairly.

In both my case and Avdi's, we could have cleared up the issue with better communication. As a team lead now, if I have a developer who is not showing up, is not responding to communication, or just generally causing workflow issues, I will try and find out the cause. Many times people have to deal with personal issues, which is fine.

You should not wait six months and then issue a punishment—as soon as problems start to manifest, open a dialogue. Find out what is wrong. Something as simple as, "Hey, I noticed you haven't been logging in regularly and were gone all day. Is everything all right?" can be enough for the person to notice that their behavior matters. I could have gone to my coworker and given him the bug report, and offered my help.

When it comes to professional matters, fostering an environment of open dialogue is a significant boon, but it's not easy. If team members are not afraid to speak up about problems, be they technical or personnel, a better resolution can be had. At my company, we have team meetings every week. After releases, we go over how well the release went. We try and root out issues instead of letting them fester.

As a team lead you not only need to find process problems but possibly personnel issues. If you notice that a team member is having a lot of negative code reviews, find out why. They may be tackling issues that are too complicated for them. In those cases, you should try and build that developer

---

[2]   On being the employee who 'needs improvement: *http://wp.me/p2NT84-2yV*

up through training, mentoring, and experience. Make sure they get issues better matching their skillset. This approach is a long term investment in improving your team's overall productivity.

If the problem cannot be democratically fixed, you may need to take more drastic action. Personal Improvement Plans, when not used as a punishment or excuse for firing, can be an excellent tool to help someone get back on track. Don't use them as punishment, and they should not be the first response to a problem. While you should never strive to make another team member feel bad, bring their behavior or lack of performance to their attention.

After you have been democratic and tried to have them help themselves, and then authoritarian by forcing help upon them, you may still have problems. There is only one final thing to do, which I hope is a difficult decision for you. Sometimes people are just not a good fit for your team and need to find other opportunities.

Communication Helps

The big takeaway with this is you need to try. Letting small issues like the above grow into massive problems can sometimes only be dealt with by a heavy hand. Inevitably, there were plenty of opportunities to correct the problems before they blew up. I find it rare that most issues cannot be fixed once everyone starts to communicate. You do not have to air your grievances or publicly shame anyone. Treat the other person like an adult.

You may need to learn to be a bit more forward for those times when it is warranted. It is helpful not only when dealing with problems, but also making sure that external issues are addressed. Related to this, recall in _Chapter 2_, I discussed how to deal with making sure your team has what it needs, which means more communicating with people, and even maybe having to be firm in what you want.

Chapter 14

The Talk

About the only thing that makes me upset as a lead developer is people that do not play ball. I am entirely for questioning authority, asking questions about workflows, and having ideas on making what we do work for everyone, but it *really* bugs me when someone doesn't even try to work with the team.

I have spent the last year and a half sharing my workflows, my ideas on how to run a team, and other topics when it comes to making sure your team is working well. I am not pulling these ideas out of thin air just for the sake of a column, but base these notes, tips, and tricks on what I have come up with other the last five years, I have been a team lead.

A time will come when you're going to have to have The Talk—the talk where you explain to someone (or a group of people) that there is a rhyme and a reason for the way you, as the lead developer, have laid things out. Whether they like it or not, your company has hired you to run the team, and you are responsible for the output of the group. If something is not working, you need to fix it.

The Talk is never a fun talk. I am the kind of manager I want to have. I do not like to micromanage people because we are all adults, and we should be able to manage our time. If you are a junior developer on my team, it is expected that you will need more hand-holding on different things,

14. The Talk

but as developers move up the ladder, I expect more out of them. If you want to be a mid or senior developer, you need to act like it.

Before The Talk

I try not to assume people are specifically going out of their way to do a lousy job. Coming up with a workflow for a team is a balancing act, and you should consider everyone's input. A good leader listens to their team, with the understanding everyone is working toward the same goal. You need to balance letting everyone work the way they want with making sure you can keep track of progress and communicate effectively.

When you have someone on your team who's not pulling their weight, outwardly or passively ignoring established workflows, or not doing the work they are assigned, the first thing is to find out why. Last month I wrote about burnout, and that can be a genuine possibility. Maybe they have been stuck working on maintenance tickets and want to do something new. Perhaps they are working with a technology stack that is just not in their wheelhouse. It could be something at home.

Find the Root Cause

First, find out what the real issue is. Talk to the coworker and see if you can find out what's going on. It will only breed resentment on the team if you immediately go on the offensive and start threatening people. I know if a manager were that way with me, I would start looking for a new job.

Take a Break

Take a mental health day. Sometimes all someone needs is a day to recharge their batteries, especially in the startup pace that many companies foster. If they have not had a vacation in a while, have the person take some time off. It may be as simple as just moving them to a new area of the code to get them out of the rut they are in.

Ask for Feedback

If it is an issue with the workflows themselves, try and get feedback. I regularly let my team know to come to me with any complaints about things. I recently introduced a new rule that all pull requests will need to have documentation and tests, which can be both unit tests and integration or behavioral tests. I made this a formal rule because we have been having quality issues recently, and I also want to reduce "my code" syndrome.

This rule is a change to our workflow, but not a major one. I will fully work with my team to make sure they follow it before resorting to punishing anyone for not following the rules. That being said, I would expect everyone to remember this new rule after a short while. If I get a pull request in three months without any documentation, I will be less forgiving then than I am right now.

Write It Down

When you start to notice a pattern and are worried a coworker may need something more forceful, begin to document these talks. I hate to say this, but part of it is for the Cover Your Ass portion of this job, but also because you want evidence of things getting better or worse. Your employee handbook, or even Human Resources, should be able to help determine what you may need to do. If things start to get better, that can quickly turn into examples of how they are doing better.

Having The Talk

If you have tried to work with the problematic coworker and nothing is working, you need to talk about their performance. This talk is intended to make it known that the coworker's actions are no longer tolerated. It's a direct acknowledgment their performance is causing an issue with the team or the project itself. For me, this means we have tried to find a way to make things work, and we need to be very real and very serious about the next steps and potential outcomes. We want to be clear that if the situation does not improve what the consequences are, up to and including if termination is on the table.

Brief Management

Before you have this talk with the coworker, make upper management aware. Depending on your company, you may or may not have the direct power to terminate someone. Still, you need to make upper management aware there is a problem, that you have tried to work on it between yourself and the coworker, and that a severe next step is being taken. In my case, I have the power to recommend who we need to terminate if it comes down to it. You may not—make sure you are working within the confines of your company.

Once the proper people know (be it a manager, or human resources, or whomever), you need to schedule this talk. I do not like to spring this specific talk on someone out of the blue. If you have been working with this person, then the meeting should not be unexpected. The intent is not to directly terminate the person, so I am perfectly fine letting them know what the meeting is about.

Have Specific Examples

You need to be prepared with concrete examples of the problems. If you started to document the times when instructions were not followed, and you attempted to correct it, you should have a good portion of this already. I hate metrics, so I never bring those up, but it can be hard to avoid without documenting specific events. For example, I am never going to punish someone because they haven't closed enough issues, but I will punish someone if they refuse to follow our merge and close procedures.

During this talk, you need to express precisely what the problem is. Saying, "Bob, things are not working out, we need to improve" is not going to help any party. You need to be specific in what the problem is, so something like, "Bob, there seems to be an issue with following our pull request workflow, and it is causing problems getting issues resolved" is much more direct. You are laying out what the issue is, and from there can come up with a plan.

14. The Talk

Personal Improvement Plans

You may want—or human resources might direct you—to come up with a Personal Improvement Plan (PIP) for this coworker. This term has a very severe and negative connotation in the business world, as it can easily be used to get rid of a troublesome employee versus its intention—as a way to help an employee correct their mistakes.

A PIP should have three parts: what outcome you want to see, how long the employee has to complete the PIP, and what the consequences are of not following the PIP. Most of the time, that consequence is termination, but there should be some sort of consequence.

A PIP should have clear goals the employee needs to meet, and a time frame to do that. If we take Bob above, we may want to say that we want to see at least 80 percent of the issues closed follow the proper process. You may shoot for 100 percent, but the idea is you want to try and work with the employee to improve. With a completed PIP, the employee should be improving without the fear of an unreachable goal.

Do not set the employee up to fail. PIPs have been used as a shield to get rid of someone by setting ultimately unrealistic goals. I find this cowardly, and any leader that does this does not deserve to be a leader. PIPs are not sticks to beat the employee with. They are meant to help the employee.

Support the Employee

Work with the employee to make sure the goals can be completed. If it requires extra training, make sure they get that training. If it means checking on them every day or having one-on-ones with them weekly, do that. You both should want to improve the situation.

This belays a bit of the problem with PIPs. Many of the issues may not have a quantifiable fix, but in the business world, you (or more likely HR) want to have a specific metric someone can point to if termination is needed. If it is an issue with the tone of code reviews, and you want Bob to be less of an…well, less aggressive, that can be hard to quantify.

This will not be an easy talk, but you can do it.

Following Through

If you set up a formal PIP or come up with something else, you need to check up on the employee regularly. Do not say, "Complete this in 90 days or else!" and then circle back around on day 89 to find nothing was improved. If you do not want someone on a team anymore, just find out what it takes to terminate an employee. Don't drag it out as it causes further issues for everyone involved, such as decreased morale, loss of respect for leadership, and even resentment among employees and higher-ups.

Part of the PIP or plan should be regular check-ins. The frequency can be weekly or daily, but keep track of what the employee is doing. If you see signs of improvement, let them know! This period should be the time where the carrot is the focus, not the threat of the stick it is attached to. We should want to give the employee the ability and the tools to do better.

If they complete the PIP, then this is a success and should hopefully correct any future problems. If someone is continually falling back into needing a PIP, then they are not a good fit for the team. For example, if you cannot follow my simple issue workflow in GitHub or ensure your work has tests and after constant work still cannot do it, then I have no recourse but to remove you from the team.

If they cannot complete the PIP, then the consequence part of the PIP comes into play, which is usually termination. If it comes to it, work with your company and the Human Resources department on what termination policies are. For most companies, this means termination is probably scheduled for Friday afternoon (or whatever the end of the week is) or possibly the next morning. Just follow through whatever that process is, knowing you tried to make the situation better. You cannot win every time.

It Sucks

It is never easy when it comes to having The Talk. I should know, I just had to have this talk recently with a few members of my team. We have had a consistent workflow for more than a year, with only minor changes like the code reviews. Things have gotten better, but we are still having problems with people not working on the issues assigned to them and going cowboy.

That means having "The Talk" and now reporting to my manager on each of those employees' status. If it comes down to it, I have the authority to recommend their termination. I do not want that to happen, but it is a real possibility.

And it sucks, and it is one part of being a team lead I hate. Try to pay attention to performance and don't let issues fester or spiral out of control. It's only harder to deal with if you put this off.

Chapter 15

Burning Out

The tech industry is a double-edged sword. On the one side, we (generally) have well-paying jobs with nice perks, but on the other, we can easily slip into not only tedious, repetitive work but figurative death marches. Most companies use the former as an offset to the latter, but that rarely works out well. This model leads many developers to come face-to-face with burnout.

Burnout in humans is much like it is in rocketry—we work hard and sometimes fast to achieve our goals, but in the end, we are completely spent. We are exhausted not only emotionally but physically, and all of our motivation can disappear. Instead of rocket fuel, the life inside of us dwindles, and we feel empty, used, and tired. This experience is not uncommon for developers.

That's all you have to look forward too. Enjoy!

Okay, okay, it is not all dreary and horrible. Burnout is a serious issue we must watch out for and combat. As an industry, we must learn to notice when burnout is happening to help each other. Burnout is unhealthy for any individual, but it will kill your team's productivity, increase turnover, and make it harder to recruit as people learn about the environment at your company.

Detecting Burnout

There are a few signs you or someone on your team may be experiencing burnout. Once we know what to look for, we can deal with the burnout issue itself.

The most significant indicator is a lack of motivation or engagement at work. To you as a lead developer, this should be a glaring indication of burnout. When burnout starts to hit, one of the first outward signs to other people is a drop in performance or attention to their work. You may notice small issues are taking longer than usual, or larger, more complicated problems are not being thought through like before.

Less visible, more emotional signs can cause a lack of motivation. Things like worrying over small details, or feeling like there is never enough time to finish work. These feelings can end up manifesting in dour thoughts, and those thoughts can quickly turn into low motivation at work. These feelings can be overshadowed by real-world situations where there is not enough time to finish something. In an environment where deadlines can be unrealistic, it may be hard to figure out if the feelings are real or just the beginnings of burnout.

Once the emotional signs start to hit, they can quickly turn into physical effects. Not only is there decreased motivation, but they can also affect people's health. Once someone starts to worry about aspects of their job, this can lead to stress, which turns into sleeplessness. Anxiety and not being able to shut off your brain at night is one of the leading causes of lack of sleep. Our bodies need sleep to recharge and allow our minds to catalog the day's events. When we do not get enough sleep, it affects us physically.

Lack of sleep can cause many physical effects—primarily, a lack of energy. When you do not sleep well, especially over weeks or months, it takes its toll on your body. You are more apt to get sick, and not with something like a cold. You can become more at risk of heart disease, obesity, and high blood pressure. The NHS[1] has a good list of things that can occur with a lack of sleep, as well as tips for better sleeping habits.

Avoiding Burnout

Now that we know what to look for, we can start to combat it before it happens, or once we begin to notice it. Everyone is different, and every person's burnout differs. Thankfully, there are many different ways we can help deal with burnout.

Take Breaks

The easiest thing to do is simply take a break. Our job is mentally taxing, and our brains need time to recharge, even throughout the day. When you start to feel like something is off, just take a break. Very few of us are in high-pressure situations day after day after day, so taking a 15-minute break is a good start. Get up, get a drink, take a walk around the office/neighborhood, take the dog/cat/hamster for a walk. Get up and stop thinking about what you are doing for 15 minutes.

---

[1]   NHS: *https://phpa.me/nhs-lack-sleep*

If you want something more structured, you can look into something like The Pomodoro Technique[2]. It's a time management technique to help you manage how long you work before a break. The short of it is this: you work on a single task for twenty-five minutes (called a Pomodoro), take a five-minute break. Repeat until you've completed four Pomodoros, then you take a more extended break, like thirty minutes. All of these breaks help keep you from being overwhelmed over a long period and help you focus better on the task at hand.

Set Working Hours

You should couple the Pomodoro technique with setting strict working hours. For many of us, we get to work at home or can work from home, which can make it very hard to effectively "stop working" once the day is done. For me, I tend to work from 9:00 am until 6:00 pm, and after that time, I try not to do any work what-so-ever. Before 9:00 am, I do not work. Having discrete start and stop times, even in a flex-time environment, can help make sure you stop thinking about work-related things right before bed.

Use Vacation

You and everyone on your team should be taking advantage of vacation time. If you do not use it, you are effectively throwing out a perk you probably fought for when getting hired. While not everyone can just say, "I'm off for a week, goodbye!" you should schedule times where you are gone and do not work. Many of the topics I have discussed in other chapters should make it easy for you or anyone to leave for a week and without having your vacation interrupted.

If you happen to work at a place that has a "no vacation limit" policy, take advantage of it (within reason). Schedule a week or a long weekend every few months, whether you think you need it or not. Do not abuse it, but vacations and longer breaks are just as crucial as taking breaks throughout the day.

The People Around Us

When you start to feel like you are burning out, talk to someone. Find at least one person you can talk about things with that will listen and support you. They can be a partner, a family member, a friend, a mentor, or someone that lets you vent about whatever is going on. It sounds somewhat hokey, but it can make things better by talking about it.

These types of social interactions are good for us, as it helps strengthen friendships and bonds. We learn that we are not the first, nor the last, to suffer from the effects of burnout. We can learn how other people dealt with or avoided it. Talking about it can take the pressure off of the issues at work, and maybe even provide some insight into what is ultimately causing the burnout.

---

[2] *The Pomodoro Technique:* *https://phpa.me/pomodoro-technique*

15. Burning Out

Hobbies

If you do not have a hobby, take one up. One large factor with burnout is the all-consuming thoughts that come from being burned out and focusing on the negative things at work. Having a hobby not directly related to your job will help take your thoughts away from something like programming and direct your energy into something else. For me, this is playing video games and watching professional wrestling. I can do these with or without other people, and they can help take my mind off things going on at work.

To a more considerable extent, find something with a social aspect. Meeting new people, or even getting together with a group of friends, is an excellent diversion from what happens at work. Many communities now have Facebook groups you can look for that share common interests. Check with your local library about groups that meet there and see if anything piques your interest. Meet up with friends and hang out, or do a structured activity. Every few weeks I meet with my friends to play tabletop roleplaying games. We may complain about our respective jobs, but really, we've disengaged so far from work we ignore it.

Get Healthy

Burnout can cause a lot of health-related side effects, but overall poor health exacerbates many of these. A job where we sit all day and flex our mental muscles does not exactly make for the most healthy of professions. It is nice to have a kitchen filled with snacks, but those snacks can be the enemy.

If you are not already, you should be doing at least some basic exercise. It can be something as simple as going for a walk every day on your break. When the weather is nice, I take my dogs on a walk twice around a section of our neighborhood. That ends up being a mile worth of walking in about twenty-five to thirty minutes. I do that for the first half of my lunch break, and then have lunch in the second half. If you don't have dogs, find ways to take a walk during your breaks instead of sitting at the computer.

If you have the time, start a real exercise routine. For the last few weeks, I have been making sure to go to the gym every morning, and I have a specific routine I follow. It does not have to be something where you work out for an hour, but you can drop in and do something on a schedule. My Wednesday routine only takes me about 40 minutes to complete, compared to Monday, which generally takes an hour.

If you do not want to get a gym membership, there are plenty of online tools you can sign up for that will help you work out at home, and many workouts do not require you to spend lots of money on equipment. For a long time, I used an online yoga program, but ultimately I am more consistent when I leave the house to work out. Each person is different, so find what works for you.

Diet is another significant factor. Eating fast food every day can take a toll on your health, and not just in the way *Super Size Me* showed. Sugars, fats, and all the stuff that goes into fast food can have a negative impact on our bodies. I love me some Chick-fil-A, but I should not eat it every single day. Try some small steps like cutting out soda, or swapping out candy for more healthy snacks like fruit. Even a simple change can have a significant impact on your overall health.

Burnout Versus Depression

On a more serious note, many signs of burnout can also be signs of depression. Exhaustion, having trouble sleeping, concentration issues, all of these can be signs of both depression and burnout. Negative thoughts can also be attributed to both, as you start to worry about the facets of your job or the project you are working on.

Depression tends to be much more general in nature. Work may be a factor in a multitude of things leading to depression. Burnout tends to affect just work (most of the time), but depression tends to take its toll on many different aspects of your life. With burnout, you may not want to go to work but want to do your hobbies. With depression, you don't want to do anything.

If you think you are suffering from depression, get help. If you are not sure where to start, Ed Finkler founded Open Sourcing Mental Illness[3], an organization that directly targets the tech industry. It is run and supported by awesome members of the PHP community as well as doctors who understand our industry.

OSMI has a ton of great resources that can help someone start to find help and deal with depression, and if you think your burnout is something more or is turning into something that is affecting your life overall, please check out OSMI.

Getting Better

When it comes to burnout, some small changes and breaks can be more than enough to start to break free from the issues that burnout creates. If you are reading this article and notice some of it rings true for members of your team, check on them. Most people do not come right out and say, "I'm burned out, so just give me a few days." Sometimes, it takes someone else to notice.

If you notice yourself starting to burn out, take action. Take a break or find a hobby. Do something to take your mind off of work for a little while. If it is a serious work situation, talk with management or supervisors about making your environment less conducive to burnout.

And no matter what, stay healthy, both physically and mentally.

---

[3] *Open Sourcing Mental Illness:* https://osmihelp.org

Chapter 16

It's Toxic

The tech industry is relatively young, and in many ways, it shows. In one of my favorite books, *Hackers: Heroes of the Computer Revolution*[1], Steven Levy talks about the birth of the open-source industry going back to the late fifties and early sixties. Many of his descriptions of programmers then are not vastly different from programmers today. These problems are not technical and can drive good programmers away. What can we do to avoid these issues?

> *"The Tech Industry. You will never find a more wretched hive of scum and villainy. We must be cautious."*
>
> – Obi-Wan Kenobi, to a junior programmer, probably.

We know the story. The lone programmer working late into the night, burning the candle at both ends as they invest themselves in whatever their passion project is, or whatever problem they are trying to solve. The caffeine-filled cups rise from the desk as a growing monument to their dedication

---

[1] Hackers: Heroes of the Computer Revolution: https://www.amazon.com/dp/1449388396

to their craft as they are awash in the pale blue glow of the monitor. They cannot stop until the problem is solved.

This programmer is abrasive, but everyone puts up with it due to the value they bring to the product. They get to play by their own rules most of the time because they are a problem solver, above the petty bureaucratic regulations which define the rest of the organization. Not only is IT the best department in the company, but the programmers are also the cream of the crop. Who cares if they look like they have not left their desk, in the basement, for the last twenty-four hours? They need some sleep, which is why he laughed at a colleague's suggestion during the meeting.

We love to romanticize many of our faults. Steven Levy writes how many early open-source developers were working near round-the-clock at the TX-0, one of the first computers which helped break away from the punch-card generation of machines. When they weren't sleeping at their desks among piles of printouts and Coke bottles, they were at Chinese restaurants solving their technical problems.

Many of these ideas can be taken to an extreme and can make an environment toxic. As a lead developer, one of the most unfortunate parts of the job is having to fight back against this romantic, yet possibly toxic, image developers have helped shape. While you should not stifle innovation, you need to make sure your team is in a healthy place.

Poor Work-Life Balance

One of the worst things an employee has to deal with is a poor work-life balance. We all love the idea of a forty-hour work week, but at the same time, many companies are trying their hardest to keep you from leaving. If you enjoy being in the building and your needs are being met, why should you go home? Inspiration can happen at any time!

I have two friends who let me tour their respective massive tech offices. The first time I heard about all the fringe benefits a particular search engine company provided on campus, it sounded amazing. They would do your laundry, and there was a restaurant serving delicious food for free, tons of places to get up and work at when you did not want to be at your desk. If you were young and didn't have a family, it would be amazing.

The second time I got to tour a major tech company, I saw the cracks. It was much the same idea. Tons of awesome amenities, but the idea was to keep you there. Work late, then eat at the on-campus restaurant, maybe put in another hour or two while traffic dies down, then leave.

I could not find the original place I read it, but one thing which sticks with me is that for a person to have a healthy life, they need to have three families and keep them balanced: a home family, a work family, and a social family. Without all three, a person begins to suffer, leading to burnout and even physical problems.

When we spend all of our time working, we neglect the other two families. Always not being home can negatively impact relationships with partners and children, snowballing into many different personal problems. Ignoring your social family removes a much-needed outlet people need in the form of social interaction, fun, and relaxation. "No TV and no beer make Homer something-something," as the saying goes—the "something-something" is "go crazy," for you non-Simpsons readers.

As an industry, we need to promote a healthy work-life balance. Make sure employees have a structured time they work, and once that time is over, they are done. Do not make employees have their work email on their personal phones. Do not expect them to put in hours after the workday is over. Let them live their lives, enjoy their hobbies, and leave work at work.

Scheduling is especially important for remote workers. It is much harder to separate work and home life when you work from home. Just because you can work late into the night does not mean you should, and you should not expect your team to put in late-night hours just because they do not have to come into an office.

For me, my day ends at 6 pm. I officially stop working and eat dinner with my family. From then until 9 pm, I hang out with the wife and kids, help with homework, and things around the house. After 9 pm is my time to watch TV, play video games, or do whatever I want that is not work-related. I set up an expectation where after 6 pm, I'm officially off the clock.

Encourage employees to take a vacation. If someone is so important the company cannot survive without them leaving for a week, you need to re-evaluate why. Let your employees not worry about work for a while, and do not bother them unless it is an extreme emergency. Even then, contacting them should be a last resort. You should be able to manage with an employee absence.

Toxic Management

Toxic management can take many forms, not the least manifesting in a poor work-life balance. Employees dealing with shifting priorities, poor planning, overly aggressive management, lazy management, and more can lead to a bad work environment.

If you have been reading this column from the beginning, you are probably getting tired of me harping on a few of these things. As a lead developer, it is your job to shield your team from poor management by being a good team lead, but do not do this at the cost of your sanity.

Try and identify the areas where management is causing friction. If it's a situation where death marches trample work-life balance, work with management to better plan on expected tasks. The longer someone works, even in a non-physical job, their productivity drops. The slog gets even worse the longer the march goes on. Remember to push back on unrealistic goals. Be firm, explain why a goal cannot be achieved in the specified amount of time, and try to find a compromise.

Constant interruptions from a micromanager can be just as bad. It takes time for a developer to get focused on a task. More so, when someone is constantly interrupting them, programmers lose the cognitive focus they built up. Make sure to deal especially with interruptions coming from outside of your team, and set boundaries for external influences like other teams trying to bypass you or different workflows.

Are your priorities continually shifting? Find out why. Sometimes it is a lack of communication between departments like sales and the development team. Sometimes it is just a plain

16. It's Toxic

misunderstanding of how development works. Work with everyone to try and stabilize what work is expected. No one enjoys finding out the thing they have been working on for three weeks is now a moot point because of something outside of their control.

If a situation is a toxic person in management who likes to flaunt their authority, or is just an overall jerk and it is impacting work, try and work it out with them directly. If this does not work, go to their superior or human resources. Do not let someone walk all over your team or you. Be specific about what the issue is with the person, and show where you tried to work things out.

First and foremost, try and find out where the management issues are and try to work to improve them. Communication goes a long way, but do not be a pushover. Your team is just as important as other departments, and having a happy team will pay big dividends in terms of productivity.

Stifling Creativity

One thing from the romantic version of a developer which is true, is we get to play wizards, using arcane incantations to stoke life from a bundle of electricity and minerals. We get to solve problems at a base level, and we should be proud of this.

If programming was nothing more than just sticking syntax together, all those old Java toolchains producing auto-generated code would have worked, and we would all be out of a job. Thankfully ninety percent of development is general problem solving—the other eight percent being cursing, the last two percent is the joy of it all working, and one percent off-by-one errors. Those toolchains were not very good at simulating the human brain's problem-solving ability.

It is partially a management problem, but we cannot stifle the creativity which comes with programming. Leads who micro-manage their team to the point of basically telling them precisely what to do makes it hard to want to solve problems. When you get yelled at for not following through with someone else's idea, even a misguided one, you have less of a reason to want to try hard.

I mention it in the April 2018[2] issue of php[architect], but make sure your team has ample time to learn new technologies, tools, and methodologies. They may not always be directly related to what your team is working on this very moment. However, the freedom to explore new ideas, workflows, and solutions to problems help alleviate some drudgery which can come from day-to-day work.

This advice does not mean let everyone do whatever they want, but do not shoot down someone's idea to solve a problem just because it uses a new tool or is a process that hasn't been done before. You may need to stop something like introducing a new language just because someone wants to learn a new language, but trying new things is not bad.

Going Green

If you want to see a real-life scenario where all of the above, and more, culminated in a not-uncommon situation in tech, The Verge ran an article about Telltale Games and how they lost their

---

[2] April 2018: https://phparch.com/magazine/2018-2/april/

developers[3]. Management practices and other things led to not only layoffs but to burn out and eventually to lose some of their most influential people who had worked on their successful games.

This, ultimately, is the best reason for you to work toward making a "green" work environment, free from as much toxicity as possible. Your team is less likely to leave when they are happy and enjoy the things they're working on. If you are hiring, having happy employees is an excellent sell for anyone new looking to come on board. It is usually much cheaper to keep an existing employee than find a new one.

When I last looked for a job, I was very upfront about work-life balance with each employer. While I would be a remote employee, I like to keep standard business hours. I was not looking for a job where I would be expected to work just because someone needed me at midnight, or dinner time, or on vacation. Anything in the job descriptions talking up all the awesome amenities the office made me look at them with a more critical eye.

Making sure your team is happy is one of the most important things you can do as a team lead. A happy team is a productive team, and a productive team is a team generally getting things done on time.

And hopefully, this makes everyone happy.

---

[3]   Telltale Games and how they lost their developers: *https://phpa.me/verge-telltale-toxic*

Chapter 17

Ongoing Education

As a development lead, one of the best things you can do for your team is encouraging and fostering an environment of ongoing learning. There is an entire world of developers out there who stagnate in their jobs because they don't learn anything new. It does not have to be a whole new language, but every developer should continuously be learning. There are a few ways you can help with this.

When my family got their first computer, it was a Tandy Color Computer III. It was one of the early model computers, which also took cartridges for programs, in addition to cassette tapes and 5 1/4 floppy disks. The disk drives were expensive, our tape deck was flaky, and we did not have many cartridges. We had all the manuals, and since this was a computer from the late 80s, the manuals were actually informative. They explained how the machine worked and even introduced basic programming—in BASIC.

If I wanted to use this computer, I would need to learn to program. Unless I wanted to learn assembly programming—which I didn't even know existed at the time—my only option was BASIC. That is precisely what I ended up doing. I spent my time pouring through the manual as well as books and magazines that had BASIC programs listed in them. I did a lot of text-based games and never really got into the graphics side of things.

17. Ongoing Education

Fast forward to 2018. Technology has moved at an incredible pace. Since the early 90s when we got the Tandy, I have learned BASIC, HTML/CSS, Perl, JavaScript, RPG ILE, COBOL, C, C++, Visual Basic 6, Visual Basic.NET, C#, PHP, Go, Python, Ruby, and I am sure there are a few others I have forgotten. I'm not tooting my own horn, but with the progression of technology, I have had to learn different things. I got into web pages in the 90s, so HTML and CSS were my jam. I ended up moving to Perl for my first paying programming job. I learned Perl out of necessity, not because I wanted to. I had a problem, and Perl was the solution.

In just the PHP space, you have to contend with a multitude of frameworks, as well as legacy code. It will not be uncommon for someone to change jobs and have to learn an entirely new framework—or learn an ancient, homegrown framework. While they are all written in PHP, each one does things in their way. Learning how to work within the expectations of different frameworks is always a win.

All the other languages I have learned have either been because of schooling or because that was the direction my problem led me in. Just recently, I chose to learn Go because it helped me solve a need for an easily compilable binary I can move between machines that included a CLI component and an HTTP API component. I *could* have done it in PHP, but Go was the better choice since it offered the ability to compile everything down into a single executable, and that one executable could be run from the command line or daemonized to serve an API. I have had to do more Python and brush the dust off that knowledge so I can understand the backend of our software better.

> *"Train people well enough so they can leave, treat them well enough so they don't want to."*
> – Richard Branson

Getting a Budget

I highly suggest working with your management team and higher-ups to set up a training budget. Having a training budget will encourage employees to pursue further training, and it is a great recruitment item when looking for new employees. In fact, the last time I went job hunting, which was less than two years ago, nearly every single company I talked to did not have a training budget, but loved the fact that I wrote technical articles, taught workshops, and spoke at conferences. They were not going to continue to pay for that, because they did not have training budgets. For me, not having a training budget is a quick way for me to dismiss a company as an employer.

There are a couple of things you should think about when setting up a training budget.

1. Don't require employees to use personal time.

I see this happen in many companies. They will gladly let you go to conferences or take time off for training, but it comes out of personal time. If you are going to set up a training budget, this needs to be factored in as a cost, and not something the employee should shoulder. Personal time off is for relaxation and time to get away, not the time for you to be learning and still technically working. Employees who are learning are still helping the company, so they should be compensated as if they were doing development. Do not penalize an employee for wanting to learn by taking away personal time. Forcing them to use their own time to learn sends a clear message: *we are not going to invest in your career.*

2. Try to budget at least one off-site training, online training, and some books.

Not everyone learns the same way. Some people will learn more quickly in a conference setting, some people by reading, and others from watching videos. As long as employees are using the training budgets, you should give them options and not restrict the types of learning the employee wants to use. You also need to be aware of your company's costs; a good rule of thumb is up to five percent of an employee's salary should be available for training.

3. Start slow but explain the benefits.

If your company seems resistant, take a step back and understand training costs money. There are still managers and higher-ups who fear that as employees learn more, it will cost them more in terms of salary or hiring costs as employees move on to bigger and better things. It is very short-sighted, but it is a concern. I am going to outline various training options, so pick and chose your battle wisely. Sometimes this is all about playing politics.

> *Two managers are talking about training their employees. The first asks, "Yeah, but what if we train them, and they just leave?" The second responds, "What if we don't train them, and they stay?"*

Conferences

Conferences are one the best things you and your team can do to expand your knowledge quickly, and you should make all your employees go to the php[architect] conferences (Writer's note—Oscar, can I have that extra check now?). In all seriousness, conferences are an excellent way for employees to learn a diverse range of topics in a short amount of time. In many cases, it is much more cost-effective than bringing in a teacher or trainer for in-person training on a single subject. At a single conference, you can learn security, DevOps, techniques, frameworks, and all sorts of things in a single weekend. If your team goes, they can each attend the talks suitable for them and share what they learned with the rest of the group.

They are not always the cheapest option, though, but there are so many conferences (or camps, in some communities) that you can usually find something to fit your budget. If you are going to try to cover conferences in your training budget, which I suggest you do, you will want to plan for:

1. Cost of the ticket
2. Hotel cost, including a day before and after the conference
3. Meals not provided by the conference or a per diem
4. Transportation costs to and from the event
5. Parking

17. Ongoing Education

The quick back-of-the-envelope math for a full week conference will probably run a single person in the area of $3,000. Now, that sounds like a lot, and it is, but that $3,000 may return much, much more in knowledge and business improvements. Using php[tek] as an example, that figure gets you two half-day workshops on various topics, and then two days of topics on just about anything you could want, and videos of all the talks given at the conference, and you'll come in under the $3,000 mark.

Conferences also allow employees to build up professional networks. Throughout my years of going to conferences and meeting new people, I know a ton of people that are smarter than me who work in different areas. If I get stuck on something, I can reach out to them. I would not have the connections I have today if not for the network I have built up by meeting people at conferences. Concurrently, growing your team's professional network can help later when your company is recruiting.

Camps

I am going to put this into its section because it is my article, and I can, and because there is a difference between full conferences and "camps." The term comes from two original conferences, one being Foo Camp, which was a sort of an invitation-only unconference, and BarCamp, which was an open-to-everyone workshop event. The Wordpress and Drupal communities especially hold their respective camps—WordCamps and DrupalCamps—all across the world in this same vein as BarCamp. In a sense, these are just smaller conferences with a much more local focus.

The Camps also tend to be much cheaper than a full conference, but at the same time, they do not provide everything a full-fledged conference might provide. Be aware, camps tend to appeal to a broad audience—not just developers, so make sure to review the list of talks before registering. Word-Camp Dayton in Dayton, Ohio, is being done in the Dayton Metro Library as opposed to a hotel or big conference center. The 2016 ticket price was $40. That is much, much cheaper than a conference ticket. It does not mean camps are any less valuable than a conference. If a local camp has things that interest your employees, encourage them to go.
There's even DayCamp4Developers[1], which puts on online conferences throughout the year so you don't need to travel.

Online Training

Online training can be an extremely cost-effective way of training and can offer a very focused training regimen for employees that need to get up-to-speed with a new technology quickly. Conferences are great, but most employees only get to go to one or maybe two a year. That means that the employee has to wait for training, which is not always feasible from a business perspective. Needs can shift quickly, and online training helps fill that gap.

Most good online training platforms will have monthly or yearly plans, as well as individual or business plans. There are plenty of high-quality training platforms out there, and you should be able

---

[1] DayCamp4Developers: https://daycamp4developers.com

to find one which fits your budget. They should also have some sort of trial that will let you see if the platform works for you and your employees, both from a technical perspective as well as a knowledge perspective.

When evaluating an online training service, there are a few things to consider. One is the breadth of the material as it pertains to your business. Laracasts is an excellent resource, but if your company uses more than PHP, it might not be the best overall option. A service like Treehouse offers various levels of PHP training as well as .NET, JavaScript, Rails, and other languages and technologies.

The second is the production quality. If the platform does not take the time to make sure its training looks and sounds good, then they probably are not spending time making sure the instruction itself is valuable. Lastly, the quality of the teacher goes a long, long way. Someone who is uncharismatic or monotone can be very offputting when trying to learn. The content might be solid, but you or an employee will not want to sit through a boring two-hour lecture.

Here are a few of the bigger players in the online training space, as well as ones that offer good PHP training:

- Pluralsight, *https://www.pluralsight.com*
- Lynda.com, *https://www.lynda.com*
- Treehouse, *https://teamtreehouse.com*
- Laracasts, *https://laracasts.com*

Dead Trees... I mean Books

Books are always an excellent go-to for technical training. While at the beginning of this chapter I harped on the speed at which things change, books provide a long-lasting resource for learning. In fact, the Python books I bought years ago come in very handy since I am stuck on Python 2.6 at work! A good programming book never really goes out of date, or at least I tell myself that to justify the bookshelves I have.

Books can be a cheap, quick way to get a helpful reference or jump start on a topic. They do not have subscriptions, and will not all of a sudden disappear if you stop paying, or a publisher decides to no longer offer it for sale. If an employee wants to purchase a book, there isn't a good reason not to let them buy it. Typically, for under $50, they can get all the information they need on a single topic. If the topic is a general programming topic, they rarely go out of date. I still reference and go back through many of my books, such as those by Joel Spolsky, Fowler, or others.

O'Reilly Safari[2] is an alternative to purchasing physical books. It allows users to browse a massive catalog of technical books online while providing note-taking resources at the same time. If you need to look at many books or want quick access to books across many different technologies, Safari might be a good option. I believe it offers online training as well, but I have never used it.

---

[2] O'Reilly Safari: *https://www.safaribooksonline.com*

17. Ongoing Education

Encouragement

No matter what type of training an employee wants to do, encourage them. Do not stifle their desire to learn a new technology, or ridicule them for needing training. Even as a senior developer, I still learn things at conferences, or pick things up from videos. New languages and tools can help bring in new ideas, so if an employee is expressing an interest in a tool or library that is a different language, let them learn it. You should balance the desire to learn with what the business needs since it might not make sense to send a developer to AWS re:Invent when you have no plans to use AWS. Attending talks outside of the business domain at a relevant conference, or doing online training, can be an easy investment in answers to future problems you might encounter.

This might also sound a bit odd, but make your employees do training in some fashion. Not everyone likes the crowd of a conference, so invest in a video platform and make sure they use it. I have worked in a few places where some people just do not want to do training at all, and while I can understand not wanting to sit at a computer and watch videos all day to learn, things change. If you need to, push your employees to train via their goals. Make it a specific goal to learn something new when designing their OKRs.

You have to stay abreast of what is going on in the space that your company works in. Not only do I have to keep up with my general programming chops, but I also have to keep up with current security trends since I work for a network security company.

Another push of encouragement is the idea of Lunch and Learns. These are days where everyone sits around and gives small presentations on things they have learned at conferences or training. Other coworkers can benefit from a single person's training, and this has the side effect of helping coworkers communicate more effectively through public speaking. It can also spark ideas or improvement in different areas the presenter might not even work on.

If your company has set up a training budget, it can help encourage employees to use it. They can quickly figure out what conferences, camps, or training platforms they can ask for without the hassle of having to ask for the budget. While they still need approval before attending, at least they will know whether or not the money has been budgeted.

Establish training as a regular part of your company. It helps your current employees grow and get better, it helps attract new talent who know they will not be prevented from learning new things, and your team can be more agile as things change.

Chapter 18

Creating a Culture

I have spent much time talking about creating and managing a working team, but there is one essential piece I've left out of the puzzle until now—creating and crafting a culture that makes people want to work on your team and stay on your team. If you have a company culture that does not attract people, employees will be hard to find.

One of the most significant factors for many developers when deciding to get or keep a new job is the culture of a company. Tech rags love to talk about what the culture of big companies are and the various ways the organizations influence those cultures. Culture is one of the few long-standing aspects of a company that drives employees and pulls in new people.

For Netflix, their culture is "People over Process." While they do offer perks like unlimited holidays, their core tenants are meant to make employees the most effective, best versions of themselves. In a company the size of Netflix, this comes directly from the top. You can find a copy of their original "Culture" slides on Slideshare.com[1].

---

[1] Slideshare.com: https://phpa.me/slideshare-netflix-culture

18. Creating a Culture

It is not my intention to recount this awesome slide deck, but I want to highlight one of the most significant slides out of the one hundred and twenty-five slides:

> *"The actual company values, as opposed to the nice sounding values, are shown by who gets rewarded, promoted, or let go."*

I want to highlight the most important things which should go into a company's culture and the things a lead developer can do on their team. Company culture starts at the top, and even if you work in a company without a great corporate culture, you can make your team better and set an example.

What Culture Is Not

I have somewhat alluded to it already with the quotes from Netflix, but the culture of a company is not the material benefits that come along with employment. Culture is not defined by the number of vacation days you get, how cheap the insurance is, or how many foosball tables are in the rec room.

There is a big difference between something like having unlimited vacation days and having a company which actually encourages employees to take a vacation. The perk belies the actual culture aspect of what "unlimited vacation" implies—something that is meant to help keep you healthy is often just used as a carrot dangled in front of you.

A company purchasing high-end hardware for its employees is a good thing, but that is not a culture thing. Any company should do whatever it can to make sure employees have the tools, be it hardware or software, they need to do their job effectively. I've worked for companies that promise "no budget" when it comes to things like that, but the culture behind that statement does not exist. I have had equipment denied due to all sorts of excuses. Or, I have had to forgo getting a tutorial ticket to a conference and get a regular ticket. Behind the scenes, someone is counting dollars, and no department wants to be seen as wasteful.

There is a term for when companies start to adopt external practices without understanding their need: "Cargo Cults." It is a term that came from World War II, where indigenous peoples would build airstrips and mock-ups of airplanes, which they equated with god-like creatures, in an attempt to get planes to land.

These peoples had no idea what an airplane was, but they saw these giant metal birds taking off and landing on these cleared strips of land. These giant metal birds and their accompanying soldiers brought with them many goods the natives had never dreamed of. It was not a far stretch to think that enticing the airplanes to land would continue this.

Many companies follow a similar pattern. Let's give everyone unlimited vacation! Put in a restaurant! Build a gym! Buy everyone three monitors!

They ignore entirely why companies put those policies in place. Unlimited vacations are meant as a way for people to feel comfortable taking time off to recharge, and not worry about having enough personal time off to take a mental health day or two. The restaurant's purpose is not necessarily just a status symbol; it is to make sure employees can have a good meal without going off campus or in the case they have to work late. The gym helps make it easier for people to stay fit. Three monitors are just dumb; it's 2018, and we should have dual widescreen monitors.

Beware companies, or turning into a company, that list those specific perks as part of their culture, and look for them to highlight the underlying benefits. Cargo cults are just as prevalent in tech companies as they were in those Pacific islands.

The Hidden Culture Wrapped in Gold

Many years ago, I was lucky enough to have a friend working at Google who let me visit to check out the Mountain View campus. I had a great time. One thing that stood out to me, and him, was how Google designed the entire campus to make you want to stay there and work. Need hardware? Just call someone. Need laundry done? There were places on campus to take care of it.

It is not uncommon to have fitness centers in larger companies, and Google had them as well. They made a big deal about how good their cafeteria was (and, in fairness, it was delicious). They had areas where you could take your laptop and have a quiet place to work or hang out in a ball pit.

Years later, I was able to visit Facebook's Menlo Park campus. It was even more in-your-face about wanting to keep you on campus. Not only did they have the same basic extras Google had, but they also had a movie theater and other things that might scratch a hobby itch. It was surreal to walk around what felt like a tiny city but was actually a company.

Both campuses were designed to make you not want to leave. If you were staying anyway, you might as well work. You love your job so much you never want to go, right? For some people, those extras are nice, but they only help drive home one important fact—the company culture is one where the company gives you everything you need, why look anywhere else?

These two companies are not cargo cults; they know precisely what they are doing. They are creating a culture that rewards and encourages "stay on campus and work" by giving employees all the amenities they need at work. For some, that is fine, but for employees with a family, it might not be a good culture fit.

Keys to a Real Company Culture

If you want to instill a real company culture, there are a few topics you should look at first. These ideas help you think about the real things that make up a company culture and bring the biggest bang for the buck. These are also inexpensive, both in terms of time and actual financial value, so they can be easier to implement without outside resources or explicit support and approval.

Communication is Key

One of the biggest stereotypes with IT and developers is this a job for people who hate to work with other people. If you want a position where you can sit and not have to deal with people, IT is where it is at! Users are dumb, and the less interaction you have with them, the better!

18. Creating a Culture

The reality is that communication is one of the most important skills for developers. Not only do developers need to have a keen aptitude for code and problem solving, but they also need to have the ability to write, the ability to talk, and the ability to express their ideas clearly. Developers also need to know how to listen to others and work with them to solve problems and complete their assigned work.

For the first element of a healthy culture, you must encourage communication. Make sure your teammates are talking together when they are working on issues. Ensure your team works with the appropriate outside groups on new features. Have your people write blog posts sharing what they've learned, either on their blog or on the corporate blog. Encourage your team to get up and speak at their local user groups. Public speaking is becoming a lost art, and being able to present to groups goes a long way in general day-to-day work and interactions.

If you take nothing else away from this article, make it this—a developer's strongest asset is their ability to communicate. Make it a cornerstone of your team and company culture.

Allow and Encourage Specialization

I like to call myself a Jack of All Trades, and I feel it is a strong suit for me. All developers should try to broaden their horizons; that does not mean you should stop developers from following their passions. You should let developers grow and succeed in the areas they feel, or you determine, are their strengths.

Having someone as the "go-to" for different areas of development can strengthen those areas; if you have someone interested in secure programming, then value and encourage their input on code reviews. If someone has a knack for designing APIs, let that be one of his or her main focuses at work. A developer who is passionate about something is someone who wants to learn and grow in a specific area.

Promote Ideas From Everyone

I'm a big fan of moving away from siloing code or areas of development, and one of the best things I think you can do as a lead developer is soliciting ideas for changes from everyone on the team. Anyone should feel comfortable enough to comment or offer suggestions on any issue.

While I just extolled the virtues of letting people specialize, there is nothing wrong with offering help or suggestions. There are many times when someone not assigned to an issue spoke up during a feature's development phase, either in a meeting or in the issue, and offered a valuable counterpoint or a different viewpoint.

There is something to be said about promoting good ideas, and it can be easy for an overzealous junior developer to step instantly. These can be useful learning moments for junior developers as they start to see how developers interact and come up with solutions.

It Is Okay to Be Wrong

Hopefully, one factor that goes into composing your team is finding people who complement each other and have been brought on for their talents in diverse areas. Everyone should also feel safe in expressing when he or she is wrong and understand that criticisms are ways to grow as a developer.

This is another crucial aspect of culture that starts at the top, even above you as a dev lead. When you make a terrible decision, own up to it. When a bug gets introduced, deal with it and do not shy away from it. Point out the mistake that was made and work with others to come up with a solution.

When someone on your team makes a mistake, you can bring it to their attention without making it a punishment. Everyone makes mistakes and, most of the time, they can easily be corrected. Unless it is a chronic problem with an employee, offer suggestions for a fix without shaming whomever to blame.

Employee Feedback

It's only fair that if I can criticize someone, they have the ability to criticize me. One of the most critical adult skills one should learn and understand is how to take constructive criticism.

If you decide to do this through peer reviews, employee feedback surveys, or some other means, allow employees to criticize those above them and afford them a safe way to do so.

There is both good criticism and bad criticism, however. Pointing out flaws just for the sake of it, doing it publicly, or just generally being mean is not criticism. Critique and feedback are something that someone can take action on and correct.

Talk With Your Team

Take some of the ideas I have given you and go back to your team. Discuss what values you want to express on your team. Write them down and start holding each other accountable.

Reward and elevate those following your team values. Show your company the values you want to encourage. Foster the change you want to see by doing it on your team. Just like everything else, culture is a team effort.

Go Forth and Run Your Team

Over this last one-plus year, I have written about a lot of different things. If you are a developer lead, I hope I have helped in at least a small way. Take everything I have talked about, and start to think about the culture you want your team to have. Make something great, even if you feel you work in a company where the culture might not be the greatest.

Be the lead developer everyone wants to work for.

Index

A

agile
  burndown charts, 12, 28
  development movement, 41
  manifesto, 25
  release schedules, 26–27, 46
  sprint, 12, 20–21, 41, 44, 71
  sprint planning, 41
  story points, 34, 71

B

backlog, 21, 26, 28–29
  list, 20
Big Design Up Front (BDUF), 24
branches, 42, 45–50, 52–53
  base, 42
  git, 47
  protected, 53
  scan, 47
budget, 4, 8, 102–3, 105–6
bugs, 4, 13, 24, 37, 40–42, 47, 49, 51, 68–69, 83, 111
  expose logic, 52
  minor, 39
  new, 40
  potential, 69
  triaging, 66
bullet journaling, 18–19
burnout, 17, 19, 84, 89–93, 96
  avoiding, 90–91
  detecting, 90

C

cargo cults, 108–9
code
  broken, 46
  bug-free, 51
  copy-pasted, 78
  deployable, 41
  legacy, 102
  producing auto-generated, 98
  pushing, 2
  siloing, 110
code owner, 53, 55
code reviews, 12, 44, 49, 51–52, 54–56, 58, 69, 78, 86–87, 110
  Crucible tool, 52
  elements, 44
  enforcement, 52
  enforcing, 54
  negative, 80
  process, 55, 74
  tools, 52–53
company
  culture, 25, 79, 107–11
  fit, 62
  values, 108
compromise, 7–8, 29, 55, 97
conferences, 2–4, 59, 61, 102–4, 106, 108
  local, 60
  online, 104
  regional, 3

D

DayCamp4Developers, 104
deadlines, 3–4, 6–7, 12, 20, 35, 40–41, 72, 90
 client, 7
 hard, 7, 66
developers, junior, 33, 58, 60, 83, 110
documentation, 32, 38, 48, 51, 66, 69, 84
 primary onboarding, 66
 technical, 58, 66
 updates, 73
 user creation, 48

E

employees
 absence, 97
 buddy, 67–69
 handbook, 85
 new, 66–69, 102
 onboarding, 63, 65–66, 68
 potential, 57–62
 remote, 99
 terminate, 85–86
 termination, 15, 85–87
estimates, 12, 28, 31–35
 combination-based, 33
 expert, 33
 formal, 33–34
 techniques, 33

G

git, 2, 21, 37, 48
 forks, 42, 45–46, 48
 master, 2, 14, 42, 46–47, 49–50
 merge, 43–44, 46, 48–49, 52–54, 85
 merging, 49–50, 52, 54
 pull requests, 2, 25, 38, 42–45, 48–49, 52, 66, 73, 84
 rebase, 48–49
 release tags, 46–47
 squash, 48
 upstream, 45–46, 48
Git Branch Model, 46
gitflow, 42, 46–47
GitHub, 2, 28, 37, 40–41, 43–44, 49, 52, 54, 69, 87
 Enterprise, 21
 Flow, 42
 project board, 25
GitLab, 21, 46, 52, 54, 56, 69
goals, technical, 75
Google, 19, 109
 Calendar, 19
 Drive, 66

H

hiring, 57–60, 62, 67, 99
 interview, 59–62
 recruiters, 60–61
hotfix, 47, 49–50
hours
 late-night, 97
 long, 27
 standard business, 99

K

Kanban, 20–21, 28

L

Laracasts, 3, 105
Leuchtturm, 18
LinkedIn, 59

M

management, 3–4, 28–29, 62, 72, 74, 85, 93, 97–98
  managers, 3, 12, 35, 41, 74, 79–80, 83–85, 87, 103
  poor, 97
  toxic, 97
  upper, 3–4, 85
Mattermost, 18
meetings, 3–4, 12, 18–20, 28, 68, 75, 85, 92, 96, 104, 110
  retrospective, 20
  standup, 28
mental health
  depression, 93
  hobbies, 92–93, 97
mentor, 1, 68, 81, 91
  buddy, 69
metrics, 12, 71–72, 75, 86
Minimum Viable Product (MVP), 25
Most Important Goals, 74
motivation, 9, 49, 89
  lack of, 90

O

Objectives and Key Results (OKRs), 66, 72–75, 106
OKRs. *See* Objectives and Key Results
onboarding
  documentation, 66
  tips, 69
Open Source Templates, 40, 44
Open Sourcing Mental Illness (OSMI), 93
O'Reilly Safari, 105
OSMI. *See* Open Sourcing Mental Illness

P

peer reviews, 74, 111
performance, 75, 78–79, 81, 85, 87, 90
  360-Degree reviews, 74
  poor, 74–76
  review, 80
performance improvement plans. *See* PIPs
Personal Improvement Plans, 75, 81, 86–87
PIPs (performance improvement plans). *See* Personal Improvement Plans
Pluralsight, 105
Pomodoro Technique, 91
Practice of Management book, 72
production, 37, 40, 78
productivity, 27, 81, 97–98
  lost, 68
  project's, 65
  team's, 45, 89
programming, 1–2, 12, 60, 92, 98, 110
project management, 4, 17, 23, 25, 29, 40, 43
prototypes, 25
Python, 60, 102, 105

Q

Quality Assurance (QA), 27–28, 32
Queueing theory, 33

R

Radical Focus book, 74
resources, human, 85–87, 98

S

scheduling, 26–27, 34, 97
   downtime, 35
Slack, 13, 18–19
sleep, 90, 96
   lack of, 90
Slideshare.com, 107
software development, 20, 24–25, 31, 35, 75
   lifecycle, 35
   progression, 75

T

tests, 26, 43–44, 48, 51, 69, 84, 87
   new, 43
   unit, 69, 73, 75, 84
training, 35, 59, 75, 81, 86, 102–6
   budget, 3, 102–3, 106
   in-person, 103
   online, 103–6
Treehouse, 105
Trello, 21
   board, 25

U

Unlimited vacations, 108

W

Waterfall Method, 24

php[architect] Books

The php[architect] series of books cover topics relevant to modern PHP programming. We offer our books in both print and digital formats. Print copy price includes free shipping to the US. Books sold digitally are available to you DRM-free in PDF, ePub, or Mobi formats for viewing on any device that supports these.

To view the complete selection of books and order a copy of your own, please visit: *http://phparch.com/books/*.

- **Web Scraping with PHP, 2nd Edition**
  By Matthew Turland
  ISBN: 978-1940111674

- **Security Principles for PHP Applications**
  By Eric Mann
  ISBN: 978-1940111612

- **Docker for Developers, 2nd Edition**
  By Chris Tankersley
  ISBN: 978-1940111568 (Print edition)

- **What's Next? Professional Development Advice**
  Edited by Oscar Merida
  ISBN: 978-1940111513

- **Functional Programing in PHP, 2nd Edition**
  By: Simon Holywell
  ISBN: 978-1940111469

- **Web Security 2016**
  Edited by Oscar Merida
  ISBN: 978-1940111414

- **Building Exceptional Sites with WordPress & Thesis**
  By Peter MacIntyre
  ISBN: 978-1940111315

- **Integrating Web Services with OAuth and PHP**
  By Matthew Frost
  ISBN: 978-1940111261

- **Zend Framework 1 to 2 Migration Guide**
  By Bart McLeod
  ISBN: 978-1940111216

- **XML Parsing with PHP**
  By John M. Stokes
  ISBN: 978-1940111162

- **Zend PHP 5 Certification Study Guide, Third Edition**
  By Davey Shafik with Ben Ramsey
  ISBN: 978-1940111100

- **Mastering the SPL Library**
  By Joshua Thijssen
  ISBN: 978-1940111001

Printed in Great Britain
by Amazon